20/20 YOU

HOW TO ACHIEVE THE PERFECT VISION TO YOUR SUCCESS

Rico Griffiths-Taitte

III Clink
Street

London | New York

Published by Clink Street Publishing 2016

Copyright © 2016

Second edition.

ISBN: 978-1-910782-85-9
E-Book: 978-1-910782-86-6

I dedicate this book to my mother, grandparents and ancestors for their strength, guidance and vision.

To Thoth, creator of his own creation and keeper of hidden knowledge.

Contents

Introduction

Oh, what a wonderful time to be alive. There are so many mutable examples of reform and transformation in these modern times that it's hard to keep up. From industrial, social and personal change, never before has there been a cleansing process quite like this time period. Great men and women have left an indelible mark throughout our history with monoliths of their endeavors. Nevertheless, there are many people who feel that the accomplishments of yesteryear are but a distant memory. We should guide those who are unaware of previous achievements so that they never forget where they came from or who pioneered our modern point of view. The past indeed holds the coordinates in opening our eyes to the future and we owe it to ourselves to have this grateful perspective so we can truly inherit the earth.

How Prosperous People See

Okay, first things first. Let's look at what prosperity means etymologically. Prosperity comes from the Latin word *prosperare*, which means causing to succeed, from the word prosperous: favorable, fortunate, or a flourishing growing intent. We are led to believe that descriptions like doing well, well-off, well-to-do, in the money, lousy rich, lucky, upper-class and opulent are words that describe successful people. However, this is a crude attempt to name the abundant success that we all hold within ourselves. I mean to say that if we just shift our perspective we can start revealing the clues to our own brilliance but we need the keys to unlock the doors to this offering. In ancient times, humble seekers of prosperity learned how to accomplish heightened states from studying esoteric knowledge. This knowledge or gnosis displayed the laws of how to be universally connected and the pillars of these principles are listed below as having:

▲ *Gratitude*
▲ *Reverence*
▲ *Productive thoughts*
▲ *Perspective*
▲ *Creativity*
▲ *Value*
▲ *Balance*
▲ *Culture of development*
▲ *Knowledge of nature*
▲ *Knowledge of self*
▲ *Knowledge of the stars*
▲ *Knowledge of the ancestors*

Prosperous people have always been the receivers of a wider intelligence and humbled themselves in search of enlightenment. The universal laws I present here in this book are not mere theories or personal guesswork; they work like magic, and as incredible as it sounds, I have seen the application of these principles literally revolutionize the lives of many people. This simple yet ancient didactic means you too can profit from using this mastery and lead a happier and more fulfilling existence with purpose.

There are of course some people who are happy just as they are and may not seek prosperity or success at all. However, once you over-stand, inner-stand and understand these ancient principles, no matter what your current perspective on life may be, your connection to universal intelligence will be greatly enhanced. Let us start the proceedings with our mindset. For example, imagine walking around in the fertile allotment of your mind where all around you is evidence of your intellectual harvest. Your harvest indicators tell you that when the time is right you can extract your produce, bring it home and consume it for your pleasure. Let us call your *produce* your **thoughts**, your *home* is your **perspective** and the way in which you *consume* your produce is your **pleasure**. **Pleasure** in this metaphor is that which you entertain and hold as true because it feels comfortable to you. You may even choose to share this pleasure with others so that they can also digest the fruits of your labor. What we produce in our thoughts predetermines our behavioral patterns and is the starting point of any human experience. The reason I am using this garden or allotment metaphor is to illustrate the seeds of our intent. Thoughts, perspective and pleasure can be associated with the phrase "food for thought" meaning that which deserves serious thinking is nourished by our intellectual stimulus. Our allotment reference is the proverbial "sowing the seeds" of how we must be accountable for what we lay down in the foundation of our being. This responsibility is mandatory in knowing more about the benefits of true prosperity. We can hear metaphors of what we consume or digest being used all the time like having a "thirst" or "hunger" for something. This indicates that what we think we need to sustain us is an illusion and we should prepare more groundwork to satisfy our spiritual cravings. What we feed our goals and dreams are also an indication of how we should cultivate our perspective. We should all strive to be more productive which in turn will reward the fruits of our thinking. In essence, how can we expect our dreams to grow if we do not tend to them in our mental garden?

Is this yet another book about how to become rich? No, no, no, far from it. There is a plethora of books that do just that, and quite successfully I might add. This book is not about catching the spiritually conscious wave because everyone thinks it's "cool" or "deep" to do so, but ask yourself this question: "How was I called to a book like this?" Entertain who gave it to you or guided you to it and for what reason. Even if you bought it yourself, surely there is a message reaching out to explore your own mystery to understand the purpose of your own existence. What are the reasons that you are being challenged to open your eyes as well as your mind? Know that at your core being your ancestors are calling out to you because they want you know something. They want to pass on the baton of truths that cannot be revealed until we first let go of the confines that we entertain. These truths are absolute, but more on that later.

Of course you know that we live in a world without absolutes and the only guarantee with our existence is constant change. However if we change our perspective and use the same view as the ancient masters of prosperity did and yield to its principles discussed in this book, two things will happen as a result.

1. *First, you will find yourself engaged in an educational process that is both liberating and priceless.*

2. *Second, you will create an indelible mastery of your destiny, your own calling and you can determine your own success with imperious confidence and enormity.*

This book is meant as an invitation to explore your purpose by trying its principles, even doubting its principles, as I did at first. So no, this is not just some book to be read for something to do! You have to do something after you read it. However, once you treat this as the road to elicit your own truth, you too will be the recipient of prosperity.

"Man may not know truth but he can embody it."

William Butler Yeats

In later chapters we will see that there are varying differences between being prosperous and being successful. We will look at the unmitigated benefits of prosperity from the perspective of the New Thought movement which caused a huge shift in prosperity consciousness. We will also look deeper into the lives of those who studied the laws of the universe and profited immensely by being abundantly knowledgeable and grateful. Gratitude not only plays a fundamental role in being prosperous, it also shows us how to become enlightened as we will see later on.

I will not give you the same rhetoric that books about wealth provide because, honestly, I think they do a sterling job of motivating people all by themselves. I will not lambast any other practices but the truth is the truth and this book is merely a suggestion on how we could start looking at our world and our position in it, that is of course, if we are in the pursuit of becoming genuinely prosperous. This is not just a self-help book, it is a reawakening of what you have always known, the first you, the real you.

This book will offer three perspectives and will guide you to see that:

▲ *You have always been brilliant and you should see your future endeavors having an impact on your life and those around you.*

▲ *Your journey thus far has largely had a puppeteer controlling you, and the source of universal knowledge is calling out to cut those strings to tell your own story with purpose.*

▲ *Your perspective is a successful evolution to reawaken your enlightened state.*

My aim here is to unravel and enhance some of the claims about how we see ourselves, otherwise known as perception. Countless books have been written and discussed about prosperity consciousness and how to obtain success; however, it's time that we take a look at the uses of authentic power and how we can become more prosperous from within. At the same time hopefully we can demystify some of the falsehoods about the riches of our minds as a hidden doctrine. It may surprise you to know that texts revealing true power were purposefully hidden to keep these truths a secret which served as a necessary adversary because a little knowledge in the wrong hands is a very dangerous thing. It's even more worrying to know that there are many diverse techniques to throw you off the scent of personal power than ever before. In ancient times these truths were only shared among initiated circles because its principles could be profitable once the student honored its origin.

I have set out to achieve one thing and that is to encourage a better outlook for you to become the ever respectful investigator into your own view of the prosperity promise. In return I sincerely hope that you reap the benefits from the laws of the fortunate. I have no intention to impose my personal views, although I will lead the charge to tell the whole story by examining the validity of our predecessors. In these chapters we will discover the ancient laws, known as keys, to allow you to be prosperous in whatever you do, from this moment on. You could choose to ignore these laws completely, but know this: it took the detachment of my retina to see my true purpose and know who I am. Prior to that, my vision wasn't my own.

"There is no truth until you decide what truth is."

Dr. Delbert Blair

Proceed with openness.

20/20
YOU

PART ONE:
Oh I See!

HOW TO ACHIEVE THE
PERFECT VISION TO YOUR SUCCESS

CHAPTER 1
My Eye Story

Eye Know!
Me, Myself and Eye
Happy New Fear
That's Mr. Wonder to You!

PART ONE:
Oh I See!

Chapter 1:

My Eye Story

It's a huge adjustment to your life when all of a sudden you can't see clearly and your vision is filled with blurred images that look like a kaleidoscope. That's exactly what happened to me when my central vision was distorted and I developed a detached retina. I have always been short-sighted since childhood and even though I was prepared to wear glasses and contact lenses for the rest of my life, what I wasn't prepared for was the life-changing experience that cost me my vision.

Eye Know!

I absolutely love drawing and as far back as I can remember drawing was the only thing that mattered to me and the only time when I showed signs of passion for anything. My mother reminded me that I have been drawing ever since I could hold a pencil in my hand. Even before I learned to walk, I drew on anything that I could get my hands on. She told me that when I was five years old I drew my first cartoon character called Kevin the Kitten complete with storyline. She also expressed how amazed she was when I drew advanced murals on my bedroom wall long before I knew what graffiti art was. I was an only child and I didn't have many friends while growing up, so I created my own friends on paper and lived vicariously through them. Drawing was escapism for me and offered a familiar world that I was accustomed to. Painting and drawing allowed me to create other worlds where I talked with inanimate objects, played jump rope with squirrels, had clouds that I could sleep in and rainbows that I could walk across. I invented my world with strange-looking people and places, even furnishing this world with my own gods. It didn't matter whether it was real or not, it was a secret refuge for me.

This refuge was amplified when my mother and I would do housework together at the weekends. We played records and would sing along to songs like Rolls Royce's *Car Wash* while sweeping the living room floor. Oh yes, we pretended to use the broom like a microphone stand as we sang and danced together. We spun each other around while dancing to "mambo" music and pretended we could salsa, as we polished table tops and cleaned from room to room. I was fortunate that she made housework fun and cleaning less of a chore. This work ethic has shown me the value of being creative, productive and having a house you could be proud of which has helped me throughout my entire life. Even to this day I still enjoy doing housework as it reminds me of my childhood. The fundamental lesson my mother taught me was respect, not just because I was helping with the household chores but it also gave me the tools to be a responsible person. I am also grateful that she showed me how music could give me rhythm and synergy with whatever I wanted in life and her teachings prepared me for my initial path towards prosperity consciousness. Being a child of the 1970s meant that, for me at least, this period held a great wealth of creativity. Music of that era had a soul which communicated emotions that didn't require a lot of logical thinking, just creative expression. When I listened to music, elaborate scenes would play out in my young impressionable mind as I became overwhelmed with ideas that poured from my liberated youth. I absolutely loved the endless realms music could offer back then. Composers of that time had a way of painting with sound that transported you where it wanted to take you. Music for me could do no wrong but nothing gave me more pleasure and freedom than when I was drawing.

My childhood dream was to design characters and work in the animation industry. At the age of 15 my art teacher recommended that I take an advanced exam prior to the other students which I did and received an accreditation. My art teacher advised that I apply to St Martin's School of Art in London as I had built up quite a substantial portfolio at home in my spare time. During the interview at St Martin's the course administrators were impressed with the quality of my work and asked me where I had done my Art Foundation Course. I was unaware of this requirement for admission and they stated that I would only be accepted after I had completed their prerequisite. I was feeling discouraged because I had no academic experience with drawing, just a natural raw talent, and we didn't have the finances that would permit me to study for the Foundation Course.

Although I was disappointed that I was unable to afford to further my education in the arts, I applied to several prestigious design companies for a placement or apprenticeship regardless. After applying for jobs in the animation world and receiving rejection after rejection, citing "no experience," my morale was low therefore I relied on word of mouth to promote my talents.

From the age of 16 to early 20s I drew countless illustrations for pretty much anyone that asked me. Then one day I was told by my cousin who worked for a local newspaper that there was an opening for a cartoonist on a part-time basis. Even though it was a part-time position I jumped at the chance and started doing weekly cartoons which gave me an extra income and the exposure that I craved. People were about to meet the characters that I entertained my whole life. I was ecstatic; the thought of doing what I loved and getting paid for it was no longer a dream. I was excited about the future and looking forward to having a career in the creative industry. I couldn't imagine doing anything else. I was able to create a world of different characters on a weekly basis together with creating illustrations for other clients whenever I had the opportunity. Although I was doing freelance work part-time it wasn't enough to live on and because life got in the way I had to hold down a full-time job as well, but at least I was drawing.

I never gave much thought to the five senses before, especially my eyesight. I had always been short-sighted and had to wear glasses, but at that time I was no different from anyone else that had taken what we see, hear, touch, taste and smell for granted. In an instant all my natural abilities were about to be tested and the way I saw the world was about to change forever.

Me, Myself and Eye

It was a Monday morning during the summer of 1998, which started off just like any other day really. As usual, I woke up, fumbled around half-asleep looking for my glasses before I went to the bathroom to get ready for work. Just as I was about to leave I would exchange my glasses for contact lenses except today was different, today my left contact was more difficult to put in my eye than normal. I finally managed to put it in then I went into the living room, when all of a sudden my left contact fell out and dropped on the floor, somewhere. Now, any contact lens wearer will tell you that when you lose a contact, you want the world to stop and nothing else seems to matter until you've found the darn thing. After 20 minutes of frustration and hunting on my hands and knees, I saw a glimmer of light shining on my contact. I knew I had missed my 7 o'clock train but I was glad that I found the contact, sterilized it, put it back into my eye and made my way to work.

I was working for a very famous store in central London in the warehouse department and when I finally got to work around 9:30 am, I started packing boxes of ordered goods ready for delivery to customers. Around 10:00 am and without any warning sign, my vision suddenly blurred. The image in my left eye was wavy and I couldn't make sense of anything. I cleaned my contact and when that did not improve my vision I immediately went to see the resident optician. After a series of tests, she could not see any signs of a problem but I was adamant that there was something definitely wrong.

For the next three days this weird image became more apparent and I had been going back and forth to the resident optician every day. The vision in my left eye was reminiscent of a hallucinogenic trip, a kaleidoscope of imagery manifested, even without my contacts this medley of colors wouldn't go away. On Friday of that week the optician told me that she still could not see what the problem was. She told me that if I felt that strongly about my impaired vision then I should go to Moorfields Eye Hospital in Old Street, East London. I was filled with much trepidation but made my way to the eye hospital, which was only half an hour away by train. When I arrived at the Outpatients Department at 11:00 am, they told me to remove the contacts from my eyes, take a number and sit down. I could barely see anything in front of me except blurred movement. There appeared to be only a few people in the waiting area so I thought that I would be out of there and back at work around 1:00 pm in time for lunch.

I waited and waited, minutes turned into hours as I was shunted around from one nurse to another, going for eye tests and having my eyes dilated, prodded and poked. Somewhere between two to three hours later I started to become frustrated wondering why it was taking so long for what I thought was a routine eye check. Then around 4:00 pm I was ushered upstairs, told to take a seat and wait for yet another consultation. I thought I saw two doctors approaching me but I guess that was just my double vision from the eye drops I had been given. I was then subjected to a couple more tests before being told to sit in the waiting area yet again. I heard my name being called and a doctor guided me into a consulting room. The doctor had a deep raspy voice as he sat me down and said, "Mr. Griffiths-Taitte, we have some good news and some bad news. The good news is that you have a detached retina in your left eye and you have a 30% chance of seeing again. It's a good thing that you came to see us today because had you left it another 24 hours you would have had permanent damage, even blindness in that eye." I said, "And that's the good news?" To which the doctor replied, "Yes, and so to the bad news. Based on your level of short-sightedness, we have to monitor your right eye as your retinal detachment happened in your left eye which was the better of the two." He then said, "Because of the severity of your condition, it would be advisable for us to keep you in and operate first thing in the morning." I was frozen with no emotion. I didn't know what to do. The doctor was still talking but I couldn't hear him clearly as my attention was elsewhere and his mumbling sounded like Charlie Brown's schoolteacher. At first I couldn't move, the news hit me as if I had just stepped out in front of a 10-ton truck. It was like being caught in the headlights and then "WHAM." There was initial pain at first and then nothing. That's all I felt, pure nothingness.

In my semiconscious state I felt anxious and confused as I didn't know what a detached retina was. I searched for answers in my head questioning how this could have happened. It seemed like the doctor was rambling and then he stopped. He must have asked me a question as I turned my head toward him and said, "Oh I'm sorry, what did you say?" Apparently he asked me if I had had an accident recently or banged my head. I couldn't make sense of what he was asking me or why he was asking that question, but he went on to explain that a detached retina can be caused by a blow to the head causing the retina to become detached. He mentioned that professional boxers can get detached retinas from direct blows to the head and also people who are very short-sighted can be prone to develop it too. I said, "No I don't recall being hit on my head or being in an accident." He then concluded that as I was so short-sighted I was one of those people in the high-risk category. Realizing that I was still confused he gave me the option of staying in the hospital overnight or coming back the next day at 6:00 am.

I was still in a state of shock and I phoned my mother to explain what had happened. She was at work and although her voice was shaking she quickly decided that nothing else was important other than coming to the hospital to support me. My mind was spinning at a rapid rate and I couldn't focus on anything, literally. Random thoughts were coming in and out of my mind. My heart pounded furiously as I assessed my situation thinking about how I could deal with all this: having a full-time job, doing freelance artwork, and six months prior I had signed up to an agency for part-time acting. I thought: What would happen if I lost my sight? Would I be able to work again or would I lose the freelance work due to my eye condition? I was thinking about all this and, just to add insult to injury, I was in a new relationship. We were in our second month together and by now I thought it was official to call her my girlfriend. I thought about whether she might leave me or that she may not be able to cope with what was happening to me. Was I being hypersensitive? Wounded with worry? I don't know. I was emotionally depleted. All manner of things were running a mile a minute through my head. I thought that all my hopes and dreams were going to be finished in an instant. Yes I know, not only was I dealt a terrible blow to my ego but also to my sanity because this was insane.

I phoned my girlfriend and told her what had happened. An hour or so passed and both my mother and my girlfriend finally arrived at the hospital where the doctors explained the situation to them. They were as shocked as I was to hear how quickly my eye had deteriorated. After we all discussed my options for the next day's operation, my girlfriend suggested that I go back to her place as she lived closest to the hospital which was convenient as my appointment was for 6:00 am on Saturday morning. When I arrived at my girlfriend's house we didn't have much of a conversation as I was in a reflective mood all evening. As I lay down on the bed I just stared at blurred images, thinking about how this could have been prevented and how I would prepare for my future. You see, for a while I was not sure what direction my career was going in. Did I want to be an artist, actor, musician? I wasn't sure what to do. I was becoming frustrated.

The next morning when I woke up it was 5:00 am and I thought: Wow, what a weird dream I had last night, I dreamed that I was losing my eyesight. The reality soon kicked in as my girlfriend said, "Hurry up babe, the taxi will be here any minute." She pulled back the curtains and I could just see enough as daylight was coming through the window. Usually, today being a Saturday, I would be doing something productive or creative but instead I was on my way to hospital for my operation. When the taxi arrived we got in and as I sat there I thought about the possibilities of something going wrong with the operation. It wasn't in my nature to be pessimistic but questions kept pounding in my head like: Would I go blind? What could I have done differently to prevent this? Why did this happen to my eyes? and Why me?

We arrived at the hospital around 5:45 am and the nurses prepared me for my operation. I remember my girlfriend held my hand as I was wheeled into the operating room. The anesthetist then gave me an injection and told me to count backwards from 100.

So I counted, 99, 98, 97... and then the only thing I remember is when I opened my eyes I could just make out the blurred smiling faces that greeted me, at least I think they were smiling. When I regained a sense of where I was, my left eye was painfully sore from the surgery. The nurses wheeled me back to the ward where my mother and girlfriend were waiting. They stayed with me for a while and just as my girlfriend was about to leave she leant over to me and whispered, "I didn't realize this until now but I love you." This was just the encouragement I needed as I equally loved her and that eased my painful situation. Later that afternoon the nurses changed the bandages and told me to rest. The nurses informed me that the operation went as well as could be expected and that I would be able to go home the very next day.

The next morning while lying in the hospital bed, my eyes were puffy and I had trouble opening them at first. I was still a little dazed and confused but I got dressed as my mother had arranged for me to be picked up and taken home. I was escorted to the reception area and while I was waiting to be discharged, I said goodbye to the nurses and thanked them for their help. The nurses gave me some leaflets about eye surgery aftercare. They also showed me how to apply the prescribed eye drops for the next three months and explained the procedure of posturing (which means lying down in one position while recuperating). Apparently it was vitally important to ensure that I got plenty of rest and administered the eye drops to help soothe the swelling. The eye drops stung like crazy and it was almost too painful to bear. I had to do this every two hours and I was instructed that under no circumstances was I to look at the computer or watch TV while I was recovering. This seemed an impossible task but the thing that frightened me the most was when the nurses informed me that if I did not adhere to a considerable amount of time resting my eyes, my vision would not be centered. It was said that the longer I postured for, the better my chances were for my left eye to return to its normal position.

As soon as I got home I went to my bedroom, lay down on my bed and cried tears of frustration. There I was lying there doing absolutely nothing, which for someone like me was soul-destroying to say the least. The doctor's voice kept replaying in my head about the detachment happening to the better eye of the two. Could this possibly happen again to my other eye? I started thinking about friends that I may never see again, beautiful sunsets that I had seen on my travels, and as an illustrator, of course, whether I could draw at all. I felt a sense of loss as I looked in the direction of my art board contemplating whether I would be able to enter the wonderful world I had created in my youth.

A few days passed and even though I was on sick leave from my day job, I still had a deadline doing my weekly cartoons for the newspaper because if I didn't do it, they would simply get another cartoonist to take my place. Drawing was almost an impossible task as my eyes were burning. I knew my pen and ink illustrations that I was about to submit from this moment on wouldn't compare to the standard I had previously achieved. There were times when as far as I was concerned the characters would not look anatomically correct and I had to ask my mother to check the drawings before faxing them to be published. Whenever I became annoyed by my disability and felt that I hadn't replicated my usual style I would sign my artwork with the word "parc" (which was crap spelt backwards) instead of putting my signature. Even though these pictures were still being published in the newspaper I felt that the pictures had no soul and, worse still, I felt that I had lost my passion for doing them. I just didn't think they were good enough and it was very hard to draw with a patch over my left eye and very short-sighted vision in my right eye.

Day after day I had to lie in one position with nothing but my thoughts to entertain me. There were times when I made no attempt to call anybody nor did I want to see anyone given my current emotions. This led to a very deep sense of anxiety so much so that I didn't want to draw ever again. After a few weeks had passed, my mother came into my room and read aloud an article that she saw in the local newspaper. It said: *"Cartoon and Illustrating Diploma course, come and learn the techniques of the experts, learn to do professional illustrations via our six-week intensive correspondence course"*. I thought: Why in the world would I do a course in cartooning when I am struggling to see regardless? She said she thought it would be a perfect opportunity to restore my love for drawing and since it was a correspondence course I didn't have to go anywhere, just submit my work through the mail. I was angry with her at first because clearly she couldn't understand what I was going through. I was apprehensive, I doubted my ability and, if I'm honest, I was a little scared. I had convinced myself that I couldn't reproduce what I used to do. I shouted aloud, "I don't have vision in my left eye and blurry vision in my right, I can only differentiate between light and dark, how is it possible to draw without two working eyes?" I then cried myself to sleep.

The next day while in my bathroom, I had crazy random thoughts like not wanting to be alive anymore as this was becoming too much for me to cope with. I was changing my eye patch and putting those dreaded drops in my eyes when all of a sudden I looked in the mirror and it was almost as if my reflection moved independently of me as it said these words: "Losing sight of your dreams is like choosing defeat." I couldn't believe it, maybe it was my imagination. I tried not to pay too much attention as my mind was open to all kinds of wild irrational thoughts. Then a couple of days later while lying down just staring at the ceiling, I heard a faint voice say something, so I shouted out, "What?" The voice I heard was just above a whisper, it was too faint to comprehend and I could barely make out what was being said but as it got louder the words "You are better than you think you are" repeated over and over again. This frightened me, I thought: Okay so now I'm hearing voices too. Whatever it was, this was a message for me to act and it gave me the motivation to follow my mother's advice and apply for the course in cartoon and illustration.

A week later I was accepted as a student based on my level of drawing skills and for the next six weeks I received weekly assignments through the mail. I squinted to try and make any image I drew a little clearer, but I found it difficult to breathe life into the characters that once begged me to come out and play. I used my imagination to create characters and scenarios which I submitted and was graded accordingly. I used my insight to guide me and trusted in my muse as I drew. My determination won over the excruciating pain and monumental headaches that I experienced on a daily basis. I created extraordinary drawings and cartoons during the course. My confidence grew as I received good feedback and comments from the tutor that was assigned to me. At the end of six weeks of assignments and a final examination I received an envelope from my tutor. My girlfriend opened it and read aloud the inscription on the certificate. She kept stalling, kind of teasing me as she read the words:

Diploma of Cartooning and Illustration
Be it known that Rico Griffiths-Taitte
has achieved the following grade:
Distinction

I was ecstatic. What an achievement, I felt like I accomplished all that and enhanced my drawing ability not by using my "eyesight" but by using my "mind sight." I mean, there I was with a blurry right eye and a patch over my left eye yet I was still able to be awarded with this qualification. Back then I knew nothing about positive thinking or the power that the mind could achieve. I became more confident as my love for drawing was coming back from its dormant state. I started to realize what I could accomplish and I was intrigued by what other possibilities awaited me if I looked at things differently.

Happy New Fear

It was New Year's Eve of 1999 and the last three months had been an ordeal with my eye situation. Even though my vision had not improved, my girlfriend and I decided to bring in the New Year with her friends at London's Embankment Bridge. On the train going to the South Bank, I noticed that something was different about my girlfriend as she wasn't being very talkative. She had her quiet moments so I thought nothing of it. Millions of people were huddled together on the Embankment in the freezing cold to watch the firework display over the river Thames. It was around five minutes to 12 midnight and excitement filled the air. Everyone was waiting to count down the last 10 seconds of 1999. It was the end of an era and I couldn't wait to start the New Year and new decade off more productively. The 10-second countdown began as everyone slowly counted the numbers backwards in unison: 10...9...8. All of a sudden my girlfriend of two years turned toward me and said, "I think we should break up"...7...6.... "What?" I couldn't quite hear what she was telling me so I said, "Say that again"...5...4. People were already beginning to get excited as the countdown got louder. My girlfriend repeated, "I don't want to go out with you anymore"...3...2...1. People were cheering and screaming, "Happy New Year! It's a new decade!" but my girl whom I had fallen in love with came closer, looked straight at me and said, "It's over." She reaffirmed what I thought she said, as I wasn't certain I had heard properly. She said it again, "I don't want to be with you anymore." I couldn't believe it, was I dreaming? I was waiting for her to break into a smile and tell me this was some kind of sick twisted New Year's joke. She had a serious look on her face and I knew that look, that's when I knew this was no joke. It was the first few seconds into the year 2000 and my relationship with her was over with no explanation. She turned away from me and her friends began to comfort her while looking at me as if they knew that this was about to happen. Yeah, they knew. I had a feeling they had known for quite some time. I didn't get the chance to bring in the New Year as I had planned and I went back to my place alone with mixed emotions. I thought: This can't be real. No, not on New Year's Eve! How was I going to start the New Year feeling rejected? Prior to this I felt like I was regaining my self-worth again and I didn't see any warning signs that my relationship was in trouble. I looked back at the last 12 months and thought: Wow, what a year, first my eye and then life throws something else at me to deal with on the first day of the new decade.

In the days that followed I kept asking myself, "When did she begin to lose interest in me?" She wasn't as supportive as before but she didn't indicate that anything was wrong. I began to feel inadequate that she left me just as things were going so well. Maybe my relationship ended because I lacked focus, I never challenged her about it. She made it perfectly clear when she called me a few days later saying she was sorry but it was what she wanted. As if that wasn't bad enough, I had just received a letter from my employers saying that due to the circumstances of my long periods of sickness, they had decided to let me go. I turned my head to the sky and said, "Great, thank you very much." I started to feel let down by everything and everyone. I knew I shouldn't have let myself be beaten by non-productive thoughts but it was increasingly difficult to find clarity. I was getting frustrated not knowing how to be in control of my life. The one thing I knew was I had a talent for drawing. That was the only thing I was certain of and the only place where I felt in control. I wanted to return to that confident state when I had completed the course, but with the addition of my relationship ending so abruptly, I began to struggle again with being creative and nothing seemed to inspire me.

After our relationship ended I recall that whenever I started to have monumental headaches I would lie down on my bed and continue posturing as I was afraid that my eye would not realign itself. On one of those days while I was lying down and listening to the TV, I remembered a program that came on around 8:00 am about an artist who taught different painting techniques. He described his world in a soft velvet-like tone. He had passion in his voice as his journey was an invitation to the beautiful landscapes he explored. The show was called *The Joy of Painting* and the artist's name was Bob Ross. There was absolute Zen mastery in his approach to painting as he invited the audience to see the blank canvas as a window to endless serene possibilities. I was euphoric as I listened to this man paint. I was able to visualize his paintings through his narrative of the world he created. I too wanted to experience that level of mastery in my own drawings. I felt a great need to express myself yet I was out of focus and feeling guilty because I knew I hadn't lived my life with purpose. I needed inspiration.

During that time there were a few friends and family members who came to visit me. Some gave me encouragement and others lent their support but the one person that I shall never forget is my cousin Nova. You see, Nova was the kind of person who spoke her mind and what she said also helped me to change my perception. My cousin Nova was a model; she was tall with sandy brown hair, beautiful butterscotch skin and blue eyes. Nova was standing in the hallway as my mother explained to her that I had a detached retina and Nova, who was always supportive of my talents but thought my success was overdue, shouted out, "A detached retina, detached retina, his whole life is detached." At that moment I knew my cousin saw that I had given up on myself. She had an assertive spirit and she "kicked down doors" to get things done. She became angry with me for going through this, not that it was my fault, but because this was indicative of how I saw things in my life where I had been walking around blinkered.

I spent the next few months going for treatments and seeing my eye consultant regularly. Over a two-year period I still required further treatment and check-ups, and during that time the doctors at the eye hospital were very surprised that there had been no improvement in my eye post-surgery. They advised me to continue making appointments every six months to monitor my eyes just to make sure that my vision had not deteriorated. I asked about corrective surgery and the doctors told me that corrective surgery was not an option as laser surgery on detached retinas was in its fetal stage and the results were unpredictable. I decided that since there was nothing else that could be done I would have to accept my condition. Having one eye with short- sighted vision and seeing a kaleidoscope image in the other was how it was going to be from now on.

After months of posturing, my left eye had finally settled back into its original position as the doctors had promised, although I could only differentiate between light and dark and had not regained my sight in my left eye. At least I had some vision in my right eye; I was grateful. It was all very well that people were encouraging me to be proactive as I was still receiving inspiring messages through the mail from friends, but I needed to change from the inside. I knew that I should do better but I didn't know how to apply myself. I had a history of being a self-confessed serial procrastinator and typically I waited for a sign. I didn't have to wait long as that sign came in the form of a blind superstar.

That's Mr. Wonder to You!

While at home recuperating and whenever I was bored with listening to the TV I would listen to music instead. I had created a few playlists of my favorite songs on my computer but this too would aggravate me, listening to the same tunes and having to get out of bed and sift through my albums. I decided to let the computer play at random and I went back to lie down on my bed and listen to whatever came next. Then one day as different albums played continuously, the first song of an album came on and it stunned me. Why were these lyrics piercing my soul? I hadn't heard this album before. The second song came on and I sat up. The words sent me into an abyss of emotions that I always wanted to convey but didn't know how. Things started to become clearer to me and it changed my whole way of seeing, even to this day. The name of that inspirational album was *Innervisions* by Stevie Wonder.

The songs scorched every one of my emotions with overwhelming sentiment. Songs like *Too High and Higher Ground* made such an indelible mark on my motive for change that I felt like I was being snatched out of my sleep state. I studied the lyrics to that album and I became relentless as I learned the meaning behind the songs. Somehow Mr. Wonder understood what I was searching for. He inspired me to not just see the muse, but how to seduce the muse herself. After I absorbed that album I remember turning the music off, going to my drawing board and sitting down in complete silence. It must have been about 10 minutes that passed before I did anything, as I was both nervous and excited at the same time. I felt my heart pounding as I reached for a pencil and started to scribble. I didn't focus on anything; I just became inspiration and let my mind take over as I started to draw. Something felt like it was granting me access to a familiar world so that I could animate life once again.

The more I began to draw, new characters were born and old characters welcomed me home with a ticker tape parade. The emotional weight that I carried instantly lifted. I realized that prior to my operation I was too dependent on what my eyes could see before me, but now, somehow, I didn't need them. I began to draw with insight and with inner vision, somehow seeing clearer. I was aware of an internal shift of my inner creativity and it felt familiar. I guess that's how Dorothy must have felt in *The Wizard of Oz* after waking up and realizing she was already home. My epiphany with listening to Stevie Wonder's uplifting musical insight greatly motivated me. From that moment on I decided to see what else I could achieve with inner guidance and trusting my intuition. I started to read self-help books and I was intrigued how I could accomplish extraordinary feats just by unlocking the power of the mind.

So now after many years of researching who I really am, I am grateful for lessons learned that started me on the road of self-discovery. All this opened doors to the wisdom of prosperous thinking. The journey that we are about to embark on has its sights firmly set on making you prosperous also. We will see throughout this book that the offerings of this knowledge were only meant for a select few. Those who decide to open their eyes to this universal intelligence will discover internal liberation. The symbol of the eye is a recurring theme when talking about this kind of freedom which is now known around the world as enlightenment. However, I'll start the proceedings by telling you this:

"In order to look at prosperity we have to change our perspective."

Rico Griffiths-Taitte

In later chapters you will acquire the same tools to see beyond your normal expectations just as the ancient masters did. There is no better place to start than at the beginning. First let us see an example of how our perception had been altered from a historical view in Plato's Allegory of the Cave.

CHAPTER 2

Seeing Is Believing

Plato's Allegory of the Cave
Return to the Cave
Sight for Sore Eyes
Lights, Camera, Distraction
The Pygmalion View

PART ONE:
Oh I See!

Chapter 2:

Seeing Is Believing

Before we talk about prosperity consciousness from the pioneers who used it to create positive thinking, I thought I would include the story about how the human vision can be beguiled via Plato's Allegory of the Cave. This well-known story illustrates an in-depth look at how we see our own existence in a world shaped by perception. This graphic tale reveals the deception of our known reality which is guided by something external of ourselves. The trick is how to decipher our own reasonable judgment through the illusion of smoke and mirrors and still communicate with our desires. This allegory is more than just a story; it acts as a precursor to the New Thought movement and is a haunting example of how our cognitive view has become disingenuous, unnatural and far from individual. To get a concept of our own perception let us decipher the etymology of the word allegory. The word allegory comes from the Latin *allegoria*. Figuratively, it is the description of one thing under the image of another, which literally translates to speaking about something else, not an actual description. Put simply, the word allegory means something that is not literal.

Plato's Allegory of the Cave

Allegory of the Cave represents our existence perceived as reality versus what is perceived as truth. It is taken from a series of dialogues from Plato's book *The Republic* that he wrote around 380 BC and it is concerned with the definition of the justice of man and the unjust man. Intellectually this is alleged to be the greatest and most influential of Plato's writings. *The Republic* portrays the conversations between Socrates, Athenians and foreigners who were discussing the meaning of justice and examining the state of existing regimes in the world. They also discussed the immortality and condition of the soul.

The Allegory of the Cave is set as a conversation between Socrates and Glaucon (Plato's brother) where Socrates asks Glaucon to imagine a cave inhabited by people who have been held prisoner since childhood. Socrates illustrates that the prisoners are unable to move as their legs are chained and held in one place. Their heads and necks are also fixed so that they are compelled to gaze at a wall in front of them. Behind the prisoners is an enormous fire and between the fire and the prisoners is a raised walkway. People walk along this wall carrying objects on their heads creating images (a bit like creating shadow puppets with your hands in front of a wall with a light shining on it). The objects would include figures and animals made of wood, stone and other materials. The prisoners cannot see the raised walkway or the people walking behind them but they watch the shadows cast by the objects not knowing they are shadows. There are also echoes which bounce off the walls from the noise produced from the walkway.

Socrates suggests to Glaucon that these prisoners would take the shadows literally to be real things and the echoes to be real sounds created by them. These reflections and noises would be their certified reality since the prisoners didn't know any different. They would become amused by the shapes and projections, agreeing in unison to a world they entertained. The general mindset would not dare question the actuality of any other view nor would it be accepted that anyone who spoke the contrary was considered "normal." The shadows on the wall represent what is natural to them but Socrates asks Glaucon to entertain what would happen if one of the prisoners is freed and permitted to stand up. Socrates offers another controversial question by asking, "Supposing someone were to show this prisoner who had been chained like the rest, the things that had cast the shadows. Would he believe what he had been shown?" Would he relate to the truth that cast the shadows over what he was used to seeing? Socrates goes on to suggest that if this same man were forced to look at the fire wouldn't he be struck blind, attempt to close his eyes or try to turn his gaze back toward the shadows on the wall? How could this man now function in his society having been shown this new view complete with wonders? Further still, what if this prisoner who been chained for so long was forcibly dragged up out of the cave, would this somehow enrage him against the people who had exposed him to this? When this man sees the sunlight for the first time he may go from anger to being distressed and unable to see clearly because he was blinded by the light. Plato goes on to analyze the mental state of this man by observing that after some time on the surface outside the cave, the freed prisoner would finally be acclimatized. He would see more and more things around him until he could look upon the sun as normal. He would understand that the sun is the source of the seasons and the years, and is aligned with all things in the visible plane.

Return to the Cave

In the final scenario Socrates asks Glaucon to consider the condition of this man if he wanted to return to the cave. How would his fellow prisoners and the condition he emerged from receive him? He would now be an outcast as he no longer depends on what is in front of his eyes. Wouldn't the general consensus be that this man went away and came back with his eyes corrupted? Everyone's opinion of him, after listening to his views about another realm, would be apprehensive if not deemed a waste of time trying to explore what was "out of the norm." This man may be accused of acting heretic, and if the masses were able to get their hands on this man, would they not kill him for attempting to mislead them?

The lessons we can take away from Plato's series of conversations is that although the story is metaphoric, it's important to acknowledge the representation of such an allegory. The external myopic view we accept in society makes us oblivious to the beauty we possess within our own body vessel. We as humans have longed for something to validate what we see without question or doubt, yet man's pursuit to achieve personal power has always been a bit hazy when trying to be all knowing and all wise. Some of our luminaries have reached unprecedented levels of enlightenment but our appetite for the need to know everything still hasn't pacified our curiosity of the path to personal freedom. What I mean is there is no quick route to enlightenment especially when you have been chained to the material world for so long. In the Allegory there lie questions that make the story impossible to ignore. Yes, it illustrates the prisoners' docile mentality, however, what is all too suspicious in the story is who are the hidden ones who constructed the façade in the first place. There are questions that deserve answering like: Who were the ones who freed the first prisoner, and what is it they knew? We should ask these questions with one raised eyebrow, hand on chin and a unanimous "hmmmm" of curiosity. Also, at a deeper level of scrutiny, we should ask that if this newfound insight was beneficial then why didn't they want to share this knowledge and in effect free everyone? Imagine how you might have reacted if you were chained to stare at a wall since childhood and then suddenly freed to see an alternative view.

Sight for Sore Eyes

They say that the eyes are the windows to the soul, which is very prophetic. Since Ancient Egyptian times the symbol of the eye has held a lot of curiosity and magic, and as our brains only interpret information as presented, it is this "window" that reveals the images we entertain. Ancient knowledge was centered heavily on the subject of the eye where the human perception was revered as sacred. Over time the power that is associated with how vision is received has since been altered and even co-opted based on manipulating how we see ourselves. The study of the eye is the key to understanding enlightenment and any inquisitive mind remotely interested in the subject will embark upon a magical journey in understanding the complexities of life. That being said, the eye represents spheres of information which is where we acclimate all manner of revelations about birth, life and death leading to our spiritual liberation. Simply put, there are cycles of magnificence in all manner of life yet if we rely only on external information to guide us, we fall into an abyss of visual ambiguity and everything becomes subjective. We base almost everything on what we think we see, instead of what we know to be real.

Our acceptance of what we perceive to be real remains a mystery until we pull back the curtain to show who the wizard is. This is interpreted in the 1939 movie *The Wizard of Oz* where the curtain is pulled back revealing the wizard's true identity. It is worth pondering who the wizards are in our own society in order to begin searching for answers for our own peace of mind. The word we are looking for here is "evidence" which by definition means "to see." We will observe what evidence we do possess in later chapters. When we think about the movie industry and the diligent objective they achieve through shifting our emotions, we can examine how they want us to feel through colors, mood, music and, hopefully, convincing acting. Whatever genre you prefer, the aim of movie-makers is to invite us on a journey that relies heavily on how our brain interprets information. For example, in comedy they depend on timing to make us laugh. It is important to get this right otherwise the desired reaction won't be achieved. Another example is the genre of suspense movies which also illustrates how playing with timing and unpredictable outcomes forms how we are expected to feel and respond. Look at Alfred Hitchcock movies and you'll see mood displayed with unbelievable brilliance certifying that our imagination is the gateway to other possibilities. The phrase "art imitating life" is a perfect observation that a creative idea can be inspired by true events. For example, it might refer to a movie that is based on a true story. The opposite is also true in the phrase "life imitating art" where something in the real world is inspired by a work of art. This prediction on our emotions is a valiant testimony to the work that the writers, directors and everyone involved in movie-making accomplish. They are worthy of a standing ovation for playing with our minds and diverting our perception of reality.

This is indicative of not just the entertainment world but how our society is constructed. Even the most intellectual among us have been at their wits' end trying to decipher what it takes to be in league with the almighty force that is the divine principle. We seem to forget the fundamental clues that our ancestors left us about being liberated. To be enlightened really isn't as difficult as we make out. We first have to unlearn all that we have learned and recognize the divine principle within ourselves. At the same time acknowledge that we have been lied to. Lied to by whom? I hear you ask. Is this more smoke and mirrors like in the film industry? Of course we can point fingers all day at who lied to us in society starting with the powers that be, but when did this lying start? Our parents did a sterling job of informing us with what little knowledge they had access to. They may have even shown signs of displaying brilliance themselves. However, we can't blame our parents for not telling us the whole story because they themselves may not have known. What we know to be true has only been handed to us via our parents from what they were also imprisoned with. Their experiences were all they had at their disposal while other more fortunate people were given the mental tools to more opportunity and a whole spectrum of liberated knowledge. The development of responsibility shows that our upbringing is seemingly influenced by our parents' perception instead of our own self-assessment.

Anyway, back to the Allegory; I hope you recognize that the prisoners in the Allegory of the Cave are us human beings. The prisoners never questioned what was before them because of fear of sounding crazy, otherwise known as being different. You see, those who challenge linear thinking are seen as a threat to normal thinking (whatever normal is). Ironically, not thinking like everyone else can also be considered as being a genius or unique. However, we should never forget that the mindset of the masses is comfortable being compliant. While the Allegory itself isn't really the whole story but rather the conversational dialogue between Socrates and Glaucon, it must be stated that the malleable mindset of man and woman can be easily beguiled. Human beings are non-pluralist about the differences in the world. I say non-pluralist because, yes, we all have differences but there is something quite wonderful about our search for cohesive tolerance for each other. That being said, it is time for us to forge ahead and adopt new ways of being globally astute or we run the risk of not profiting from how culturally and spiritually rich we all could be.

Even though Plato's Allegory was written around 380 BC it was, and still is, a red flag to the state of human kind. It could also be a proleptic warning asking us to not be so tunnel-visioned about our existence today. Our perceptual limitations form our personality as does our faith and even our personal view of the afterlife. However, the question still remains: When will we have access to our internal strategy without fear of being persecuted? We should all have the right to choose whatever we wish to entertain as real, although it must be said that the contingency of whether something is real or not isn't without controversy. For example, ask anybody what is the color of grass and you will get a resounding common answer of the color green. Also ask what color is the sky, and again you would be hard pushed to hear anything other than the color blue, of course, everybody knows that, don't they? But how do we know that grass is green or that the sky is blue for sure? Consider this: if we asked someone with a metaphysical mindset this same question about color they may answer by stating, "The color of grass or the sky is whatever color you want it to be." Very rarely would you hear that answer from the norm, but isn't that the truth? In the proverbial movie theater screen of our mind, Plato's story illustrates this perfectly. Our own level of conscious agreement betrays our emotions. Put simply, mainstream thinking wins hands down. Why question if the grass is green or that the sky is blue? Everyone else around you will unanimously state a unified view. However, just like in the Allegory of the Cave story, consider these questions:

▲ *How would you have acted once you left the cave of your comfortable mindset and decided to see things differently?*

▲ *How would you expect everyone around you to receive the news of what you have been shown?*

▲ *How would you behave in the known world once you returned?*

Since I mentioned the movie industry earlier, it's worth stating here the great responsibility of the movie-maker's intention that relies on our emotions and reactions. Through movies we are transported into other realms of perception and immerse ourselves in someone else's view or idea of how we live. This is classically known as escapism which alleviates our own existence. This is more than just for entertainment value as many movies have messages and stories that often change the way we look at things. Movies have topics that are relative to our own lives offering opportunities to see things in a completely different way. They are also a great way to look into characters that remind us of ourselves or someone we can relate to so we can benefit from its lessons.

Next we will see an example of such a movie that provided immense teachings of the human condition and broke all levels of perception and cinema agility. This movie is a phenomenal beacon of light about how we perceive the known and unknown universe. It is an eye-opener that invites us to travel through the eyes of human endeavor and visual acuity. It also augmented everything to do with enlightenment and that movie was called *The Matrix*.

Lights, Camera, Distraction

In 1999 a movie was released that was the best cinematic example of how we perceive our known existence which also set a new precedence in the land of movie-making. *The Matrix* broke so many boundaries of perception that it just might be the best modern day example of revealing the veil of illusion known as reality. I remember watching this movie repeatedly, analyzing its content, cinematic prowess and message. What I found most inspiring was the fact that it was very specific in its warning. Yes, warning. This warning overtly reveals that we are all born into bondage and will continue to feel arrested unless we ourselves regain our own consciousness.

I need not remind you of the plot; however, I, like many others, identified with the character Neo. When I was in my early 20s I knew intrinsically that something was not quite right with the world as it was presented, nor was I happy with my own version of reality. This was echoed for me in the scene where Morpheus said to Neo in their first meeting, "You're here because you know something. What you know you can't explain, but you feel it. You've felt it your entire life." I mention this now iconic phrase by Laurence Fishburne who played Morpheus because *The Matrix* had entirely and successfully revealed what it means to believe in your internal abilities instead of relying on external projections. I watched the movie again while writing this book and I particularly loved the line where Neo wakes up in the ship (the Nebuchadnezzar, named after the Biblical Babylonian king) and asks, "Why do my eyes hurt?" to which Morpheus replies, "Because you never used them before."

This revelation is tantamount to how many of us walk around in a mesmeric state, as we humans cannot really qualify what we see. It is without doubt that our eyes see the external world as constructed for us instead of viewing it from our own perspective. This is all very well, although more often than not the messages in movies, whether hidden or visible, can have profound examples of truth, just like *The Matrix*. However, if you aspire for change in your life, it clearly starts with you deciding that you need something or someone to show you the way. You have the choice to live a life of unprovoked comfortable ignorance or you can choose a path that marries your body, which is just a vessel, with your soul's purpose.

The veil of illusion has long been constructed and pulled over our eyes, comforting new generations to follow suit. As I said, *The Matrix* movie paved the way for people to take a look at who they really are, yet the movie's message only echoed other brilliant cinematic examples of visual entrapment. A year prior to *The Matrix*, there was a movie called *The Truman Show* (1998) which had just as much impact into the powerful revelations of our known world artifice. *The Truman Show* is about a man (Jim Carrey) who lives his entire life in front of cameras for a TV show entitled The Truman

Show. Truman is filmed through thousands of hidden cameras 24 hours a day, seven days a week, and broadcast live, allowing the world to tune in and see every aspect of his life. His curiosity was raised when daily events were repeated and he began to question who was the puppet-master controlling his existence. This scenario is relative to the experiences we saw earlier in this chapter in Plato's Allegory of the Cave.

Another movie that had the same impact as *The Matrix* mind perception was the 2011 movie *Limitless*. The movie had opened endless possibilities of what the mind can achieve once unhinged by an organized system. Okay, so the limitless mind power was elicited with a concentrated pill, but the message is very clear: look at what you can access with your mind being opened unequivocally. When the main character Eddie takes the pill for the first time in the movie, he says, "I was blind but now I see." This is very synonymous with how people have described achieving enlightenment. That enlightened state starts in our childhood as we have a malleable mind that has limitless opportunities because as children there are no restrictions or commitments that we have as adults. Movies that highlight our social perception will undoubtedly continue long into the future because of this particular subject matter.

The Pygmalion View

I am a great admirer of the works by George Bernard Shaw and I find myself returning to his plays time and time again to gain a satirist point of view on humanity. I am particularly drawn to the adaptation of the 1913 play *Pygmalion*. The play was fantastically written about the ambiguity between the social middle class strata and contradiction between the sexes. This proved to be one of Shaw's greatest successes on the stage and was later recreated into a movie of the same name.

The movie centers on a conceited language professor who tricks his snobby peers by teaching a girl from the gutter to behave like a lady and pass for a duchess. The movie was nominated for a Best Picture Academy Award, and won Best Screenplay (written by George Bernard Shaw and adapted by Ian Dalrymple). The play was later remade in the 1964 movie *My Fair Lady* starring Audrey Hepburn and Rex Harrison. The Pygmalion theme is loosely adapted around the Greek myth in which Pygmalion was a sculptor who fell in love with a statue that he had carved out of ivory.

As legend has it, Pygmalion was not enamored with the women he saw around him and likened them to prostitutes; therefore he created a statue which looked so realistic that he fell in love with it. He then made offerings at the altar of Venus and quietly wished that his ivory sculpture would be changed into a real woman. When Pygmalion returned home, he kissed his ivory statue and found that its lips felt warm. He kissed it again and touched her breasts with his hand and found that the ivory felt like a real woman, which meant that Venus had granted Pygmalion's wish. Pygmalion married the ivory sculpture which had come to life, and together they had a son, Paphos, from whom the island of Cyprus in Greece is derived.

The transformation of inanimate objects or even people's social status into something else has had its story remade many times, as in the 1883 children's novel *The Adventures of Pinocchio* by Carlo Collodi and the 1940 movie *Pinocchio*. The story was repeated again in the 1987 movie *Mannequin* starring Kim Cattrall and in the 1983 movie *Trading Places* starring Dan Aykroyd and Eddie Murphy and also in the movie *SimOne* starring Al Pacino. All of these movies borrowed heavily from the Pygmalion story.

My interest in the story of Pygmalion is purely from a metaphysical viewpoint which perfectly reveals that when you have unwavering faith at the altar of your imagination, as Pygmalion did, you can breathe life into your vision and manifest it.

"Life isn't about finding yourself,
life is about creating yourself."

George Bernard Shaw

CHAPTER 3

More Than Meets
The Eye

The Child in Your Eyes

The Four Eyes of Empowerment

How Not To Look Back
When Looking Forward

PART ONE:
Oh I See!

Chapter 3:

More Than Meets The Eye

The imagination used in movies like *Pinocchio*, and indeed cartoons in general, shows us that we could benefit from adopting a child-like mentality replete with being naturally creative. When we look at the mind of a child, we see that it is a wonderful blank canvas, which allows parents to teach their children how to interact in our society and assist with their ability to communicate. However, that blank canvas is often guided into a system which is globally filtered with pandemic timing. Contemporary trends spread like wildfire, especially in the family dynamic of raising children but in ancient times it was culture that had always been the proven formula in keeping any lineage productive. This is apparent when we look at the cultural development and societal grooming around the world by inserting a code of conduct from a very early age. Our environment is the integral component of a child's development in order to initiate them with values so that they can grow up into a productive society. Failure to do so plants the seed of unknown knowledge of self and the cultural tools that the parents invest in will struggle to harvest a prosperous journey into the child becoming a responsible adult.

The Child In Your Eyes

I for one am pleasantly surprised that amidst the cabal techniques to lead us away from the truth, people are asking more and more questions about the meaning of their existence. We should applaud those who have taken up the gauntlet to find their own truths with a unanimous "hoorah," yet be saddened by the success of an Orwellian agreement. What agreement is that, do you ask? Well, the agenda is quite clear to see how the agreement of control has guided our young to suckle on having instant gratification without reproach. In light of this let us ask ourselves a question that must disturb even the most Neo-puritan of parents. When did the modern day mind of a child become exposed to the "all that glitters must be gold" scenario without our intervention? I ask this because I once saw a mother on a bus give her crying baby a cell phone to play with to soothe its whimpering. A child having a cell phone in this modern age didn't surprise me; however, watching this baby sucking the phone and witnessing how quickly it stopped crying did elicit uneasiness. This is a perfect example of how our vision has been given a new pacifier via things that interrupt our natural emotions. Upon seeing this baby being transfixed by the lights of the phone, I reminded myself of the chorus line from the prophet Marvin Gaye singing his song *What's Going On?*

Children have a unique ability to absorb information through an impartial intellect. They tap into frequencies and have access to realms that most of us have abandoned as adults. Yet all too often we are witnessing these little darlings run riot with a hasty need to be precocious. I can hear the mothers of babies in pageants screaming, "What's wrong with that?" What's wrong is that in ancient times a child was in preparatory mode for the responsibilities that awaited them throughout life. They were taught family values and the virtues of nature, along with the use of physical and mental prowess. Respect was a fundamental life skill in becoming a holistic being.

Even in Victorian times, to encourage discipline it was expected for children to be seen and not heard and this need of obedience shaped how you would conduct yourself later on in adulthood. All of this led to a prosperous life, which has been lost in today's modern climate. If this is true then we must ask ourselves one question: What happened? Because something definitely happened.

Well, in this book we will see that the answers do not relegate themselves to just children. The answer is that the world's view has changed, expectations have changed, our pursuits have changed and so too our values. We live in a society that teaches its young to be dependent on the satisfaction of the senses. It may have always been this way; however, in these modern times our senses are noticeably focused on achieving celebrity status via the attraction of looks, money, status and the insatiable pursuit of fame.

The Four Eyes Of Empowerment

Life is very strange indeed; even stranger are the challenges that life throws at us on a daily basis. For most of our lives we are in battle mode, on-guard, prepared, getting ready or whatever you want to call it; even before we leave our homes we fight with our children, fight with each other, even fight with our hair (I'm bald so I don't speak from personal experience). We are also bombarded by the news that confronts us from the TV and radio. While we are on our way to work, there's pushing and shoving or being shoved, well before we arrive at our positions armed with the weapons known as skill-set to face our jobs. We are conditioned to acknowledge that at some point during our lives we entertain conflict from every angle, leading us to feel tension. When we use words that describe how we see our lives like battle mode, fighting, bombarded, conflict and tension, they provide us with a perspective that shapes our outlook and how we behave. We must be aware that using these words only serves to paralyze our progressive mindset. We must decide that if we are seeking a more prosperous way of living, then we have to be responsible for the way we entertain those denotations within our mental language.

Let's use the scenario of losing your job to illustrate the difference in our mental dialogue which can be seen as non-productive versus a prosperous view.

The non-productive view: I've just lost my job! What am I going to do? I can't... I don't have.... There is no time.... What if I fail? I can't retrain....

Losing your job can be daunting news for anyone to hear; however, in these times of economic reshuffling there is an obvious and natural cause for concern but let's look at this another way.

The prosperous view: Great news! I've just lost my job and maybe now I'll have the time to reinvent myself. I need the time to focus on me and take care of things that demand my attention. The loss of your job could be just the push and the motivation that you needed to discover who you are, where your real talents lie or, for example, the time to start your own business. The difference between these two approaches is mindset. A non-productive person would emerge as a worrier and a prosperous person would emerge as a warrior. Since this book is about how we see perspective and prosperity in ourselves, I would like to share with you a system that I have devised so that you can awaken your internal and external power by controlling your perception to see with prosperous eyes. If you follow these steps guided by ancient wisdom you will certainly accelerate your learning much quicker than when I started my own journey of self-discovery. I call this:

The Four Eyes of Empowerment.

Eye 1 - Idea

This is where your creative self is born. The origin of the word idea is Latin, which means the picture in your mind, a concept and being able to see. To manifest and illustrate an idea it first has to be entertained in your mind. An idea isn't an actual thing, it's your imagination. The fun begins when you allow your brain to wander as it races to find an image that you can relate to. Remind yourself how much of a great idea you are as a person – not just the way you look, but how you are able to create and recreate yourself as a character. If you find that you rely on logical thinking and you are not really creative, then it is suggested that you should do something which enhances your creative side; for example, learn to play an instrument, take an advanced class in cooking, learn to salsa, learn to juggle, whatever you decide to do. It would benefit us greatly if we can demonstrate a more creative side of who we are in order to be creatively liberated.

Eye 2 - Inspire

Inspire originates from the Latin word meaning "blow into something." With the breath of our actions we can breathe life into an idea and animate our imagination. A movie, a word, or even a person can inspire creativity in you. Successful people have cited that something or someone inspired them to greatness. Transformational change within all of us starts with inspiration. Life is temporary and nothing is permanent because everything evolves, which tells us that the lessons we pick up on our journey through life should inspire new ways of looking at ourselves.

Eye 3 - Improvement

This is a powerful word, which means getting better at something. To make something better often starts with a realization that something needs our attention, not that something is wrong. Looking at something another way can have a greater Impact. For example, when we eat more sensibly we are improving our health and when we have a good night's sleep we improve our alertness. Improving is the thinking process of creating space and not confined to one aspect. An artist can decide when their piece of work is finished and even then they may feel that they want to improve upon the work if they so desire. We read to be informed and improve our knowledge and we are never too good at something that we can't improve and be great.

Eye 4 - Influence

Influence refers to the power of a person or a thing that can affect a result. This is very different from inspiration as inspiration gives birth to creativity. You can entertain many things but influence is the flowing action from inspired thought. Having influence over your thoughts causes changes within you. As children we needed influence from our parents to show us how to do things, and even in our working environment we need influence to maintain our productivity. As stated above, we should be looking at improving ourselves but this should only be attempted if our influence is balanced in all of our actions.

The four eyes of empowerment can be looked at separately but it has even more potency when you combine all of its facets, giving you a better outlook on any situation, from personal to business, casual to professional. When we see it as a cycle, our view can define how to see ourselves. For example, you can have an **idea** to **influence** something, influence leads to **inspiration** which in turn **improves** your inspiration that leads to another idea etc.

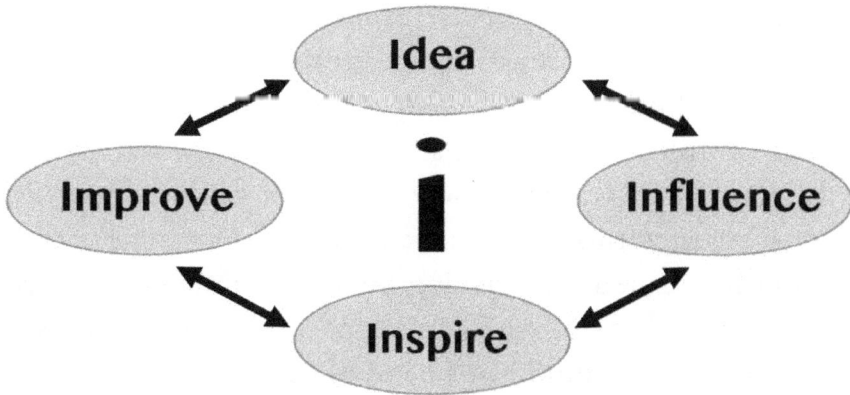

Do you get the picture? The letter "I" at the beginning of these words is the common bond between you and the entire universe. The "I" represents the number 1 as the first thought upon your initial being as the "I am that I am." The I, the self, the main contender is the cosmic brilliance of knowing that all is within you.

How Not To Look Back When Looking Forward

A very close friend of mine was an entrepreneur and brilliant artist and he had such a presence about him that people often complimented him on his aura. He was the kind of man that when he walked into a room people would gravitate toward him. He had a swagger in his walk. He was full of confidence and the look on his face always had a cheeky grin displaying his wicked sense of humor. He was quick-witted and at every social gathering he always turned up fashionably late. People would listen intently to his stories as his words echoed with whimsy and graphic imagery of his exploits. He wore the finest suits with an overcoat draped over his shoulders that accented his debonair look. He had aspirations of traveling around the world being inspired by different experiences, and as an artist he envisioned painting beautiful landscapes for the rest of his life.

Then one day he met a beautiful woman who doted on him and loved him like no other woman ever had before. To complete their wonderful life they got married, set up a home together and sure enough had a child on the way. My friend was focused on making a success of his newfound relationship and poured everything into this new life. I was extremely happy for him and married life seemed to agree with his new persona to the point where he had everything he wanted, and having a child complemented his new outlook. I remember not seeing much of him at social events and it was obvious that he could not be exactly as he was before because now he was "settled."

A few years passed and I had not seen him so I assumed that he was living his life as he intended. You see, he had always insisted that his dream was to settle down in a hot country. One day, out of the blue, I remember walking down the road and heard a man call out my name. I didn't recognize him at first then I realized that it was my friend that I have been telling you about. I could hardly believe it: gone was the light in his eyes, the aura of magnificence, the cheeky grin and the swagger in his walk. We sat down to have coffee together and I asked him what was happening in his life. He said that his wife had left him because she felt she had made a terrible mistake in marrying him. I listened intently to the way my friend described the amount of effort he had put into ensuring that he made his wife happy. He used to talk about her with such devotion, describing her as his soul mate and how much she completed him. He now spoke with the utmost resentment and anger in his voice as he mentioned that he regretted not following his dreams of being a traveling artist. He repeatedly said that she knew what she was doing to him as if she had a premeditated plan to destroy him. I found it interesting that he said he felt lost and didn't know where to turn. He said that he felt stupid and betrayed because he had given up everything for her. According to my friend, the potential man she fell in love with, who had all trimmings of a famous socialite, decided to get a regular job to support his new family and wasn't painting anymore. He went on to say that apparently she left him not only because she had feelings for someone else, but because she fell out of love with the person he had evolved into. The saddest thing for me to hear was that he was no longer painting and it was the furthest thing from his mind. He admitted that he channeled his energy into being supportive to her but in doing so he lost who he was, citing, "I thought I was doing the right thing."

This scenario can be quite typical in some relationships. In essence, my friend illustrated perfectly what can happen when we lose focus of ourselves without seeing the bigger picture. But wait! Do not look for a sad ending to this story because there isn't one, just an observation. Five years after his divorce and some deep soul-searching, my friend realized that everything on planet Earth is a lesson. He reminded himself of his ambitions, picked up from where he left off and started painting again, and by all accounts he is much happier than ever before. Yes he learned the harsh realities of self-discovery and even though it took him five years to do so, it didn't matter. He became more knowledgeable about who he was and how to look forward to the rest of his life. Oh yeah, he met a new girl, also a fellow artist and planned to marry.

Relationships are complicated at the best of times and sometimes unpredictable. The fact that we have problems is natural. How we respond to our problems is what really matters because it shows us who we are. Good, bad or indifferent we have the potential to better ourselves. When you learn to have a new perspective of yourself it allows you always to be prepared as you look ahead at your goals and never look back with regret, no matter what a relationship throws at you.

LOOK OUT: We can see that even during a seemingly healthy relationship there can be times when it all goes unexpectedly wrong and we can feel a lack of self-worth and abandoned. Loss of oneself is one of the greatest feelings of detachment. Your feelings are important and there is no "just getting over it." It's obvious that you now have an important decision to make about getting that support network around you. This can come in the form of friends, counseling or emotional support to help you emerge as a better person with even more knowledge about yourself.

PERSPECTIVE: It is better to focus on what you need so you can avoid these non-productive energies interrupting your spiritual growth. Learning to let go of people, places and events that do not serve you means that you can begin to lick your wounds and create your own attractive space, especially in finding true love, better companionship and the universal respect that you deserve.

"Never allow someone to be your priority while allowing yourself to be their option."

Mark Twain

I have illustrated some methods you could use to facilitate your higher learning with The Four Eyes of Empowerment, but in order for us to proceed in developing our perspective let's see where this prosperous thought was first cultivated.

20/20 YOU

PART TWO:

They Came,
They Saw,
They Conquered

HOW TO ACHIEVE THE
PERFECT VISION TO YOUR SUCCESS

New Eyes, Old Ideas

Gazing at the Past
The New Thought Movement
Is There a Blueprint for Getting Rich?
Meet the Fillmores

PART TWO:
They Came, They Saw, They Conquered

Chapter 4:

New Eyes,
Old Ideas

The knowledge we will unravel in this chapter reveals how we can designate where prosperity consciousness came from in terms of its origins and how it developed into a worldwide phenomenon. The wisdom of this new way of thinking wasn't really new because since Predynastic Egyptian times this knowledge was passed down through generations and only revealed to a student once they reached a certain age. However, in telling our story about prosperity and perception, we need to have the complete insight to achieve the same greatness that our luminaries did. Throughout our history this information wasn't readily available to everyone because not everyone could handle the responsibility that this power possessed. Students from the western world who honored ancient teachings and practices from the East saw the benefits of what the mind could achieve. They knew that the prerequisite for the rewards of this consciousness was having patience and an openness to learn about the universe without reproach. It's worth stating here that past and present gurus were aware that everyone has equal access to this intelligence, we just have to want it badly enough.

I could never understand that phrase "to want something badly enough" or the saying "how bad do you want it?" Surely you would want something good enough? NO! Okay, swiftly moving on.

We can understand the reasons why the road to intelligence had its tracks well hidden, although once someone was fully open to this power it was thought that this knowledge was often hidden in plain sight. If this is true, why do some people go searching for it, and why hide it or make it appear so difficult to excavate the genius within us? Wasn't everyone supposed to have access and prosper from these schools of thought? Our ancient masters seemed to think so! The answers lie in future chapters where we will acquire the necessary tools that preserved this knowing until one was ready.

Before we see the rewards of acquiring this knowledge, it's worth doing a little digging to see the historical evidence from the pioneers who used it to become enlightened. I said earlier that the knowledge was hidden with good reason, but what reason could that be? It seems that over time there needed to be control of this knowledge but how would that be beneficial and who would benefit from it? The answer is in the state of the world today which shows that knowledge is the only thing that separates us, especially knowledge of ourselves. The proponents of universal law have been inspired in discovering endless possibilities that the mind can offer. Prosperity meant having this knowledge would connect you with divine intelligence allowing you to master yourself, which was greatly seized over time. In order to explore the realms of how to be prosperous, let us look at those who altered its origins and tailored it to suit a particular time period.

Here we aim to grasp who changed the original laws and why.

Gazing at the Past

At the turn of the century many people that synthesized with prosperity consciousness were from Christian Science backgrounds. They drove themselves into controversial states trying to understand how the mind works, and at the same time the effects from esoteric knowledge were met with great curiosity. It is well documented that the most famous protagonist of any esoteric knowledge was Franz Anton Mesmer. Franz Anton Mesmer (1734-1815) was born in Germany and studied medicine at the University of Vienna. He had been exposed to the works of Paracelsus who himself was an alchemist and occult philosopher who theorized ancient teachings of the mind. There have been countless books written on Mesmer's life and times, and his theories have been studied, tried and tested, even discredited and dismissed by his peers without good reason. The 1994 movie simply entitled Mesmer, starring Alan Rickman, had an insider's look at the uphill battle Mesmer faced from his contemporaries because of his views on how the mind could alter our state.

Mesmer dealt with much scrutiny and major opposition trying to convince doctors and the scientific fraternity of his process. It angered him that their medieval ways were in fact spurious and ineffective. He believed that any ailment present in humans was largely an imagined affliction. He cited that there is an abundant supply of invisible fluid using universal energy, which he called "animal magnetism." This magnetism he cited as being an inordinate supply of power which could cure any ailment, even blindness. He would demonstrate this by placing patients in a hypnotic state, and once he connected with them and the disease they suffered from, he would then cure his patient through aligning himself with the moon and planetary energies. His application of trance-induced healing was later termed "mesmerism." He had often performed these physiological phenomena in front of an audience of his peers, which was received as some kind of trickery, and thus he was persecuted.

There were, however, many who sought to capitalize on Mesmer's applications and although their techniques were different, they were just as effective. Followers of Mesmer borrowed from his teachings and refined the approach to ancient knowledge. Most notably was Phineas Quimby (1802-66) who was a student of Mesmer and one of the earliest instigators of the New Thought movement. He learned mesmerism and set out to treat patients under his own version of trance-induced hypnosis with much success. Although Quimby was an advocate mesmerist, he was instrumental in the corruption of it also. He sought to use the Christian Science methods of healing to lure modern Americans to religious affiliations and the birth of a new way of being. One of Quimby's students was Mary Baker Eddy who went on to found the Christian Science movement. Mary Eddy did not acknowledge any reliance on Quimby for her ideas because she herself was a radical and fought to gain her right as a mesmerist healer as well. She passed the baton of this brilliance on to one of her star students named Emma Curtis Hopkins. Are you beginning to see how the cultivation of this knowledge had started to attract greed and plagiarism? Mind cure was something new and not openly discussed, however it was becoming popular.

The New Thought Movement

The New Thought movement was exclusively built on changing people's perspectives and owes much to Mesmer for his revelations. The movement originated in America around the turn of the 19th century and its fundamental teachings were in the religious Christian Sciences and metaphysics. Christian Science flourished in Middle America as big cities were going through economic change. Major groups existed around the world with their own take on spirituality and yet America was steeped in the Unity Church and Divine Sciences. As people started becoming aware of other cultures globally, it was evident that exposure to how other people lived, and their denominations were also causing intrigue. Many people were turning to the East as their curiosity grew and those from a staunch Christian Science background even toyed with transcendental meditation for re-awakening spirituality at that time. Calling these ideas New Thought was seen as old Christian faiths that received a much-needed overhaul due to the industrialization of America. There was no intention to remove the demiurge completely, just exemplify that personal power could be accessed at the seat of your own consciousness.

When prosperity consciousness really took flight during the 1930s many luminaries extolled the virtues of what it meant to be in touch with the Divine. Since predecessors such as Phineas Quimby who supported the New Thought movement, a new era of thought fused a new outlook on faith that was supported by a brilliant "How to" manual. The manual expressed personal and ancient spiritual empowerment and had the same principles as the New Thought movement. This manual changed the course of personal gain and was called *The Master Key System*, scribed by Charles F. Haanel in 1917. *The Master Key System* is a quintessential study in personal power, metaphysics and prosperity consciousness and is set out as a study course to achieve any purpose the reader desires. It was one of the first books to illustrate the Law of Attraction, which is derived from the seven Hermetic laws stated in the Kyballion. The key element when administering the rules in *The Master Key System* is to process the universal energy which is all around us to create abundance and wealth by altering your state of mind. It is well documented in *The Master Key System* that using the power of the mind determines our reality and it is also thought that it should be used creatively and constructively to achieve enlightenment. Those that read this book began to develop a thirst to know more about the secrets of personal power and they started to migrate away from the mesmerist teachings in exchange for the keys to construct their own blueprint for success.

Is There a Blueprint for Getting Rich?

The annals of wanting more for ourselves have produced thousands of books and manuals which have influenced our modern pursuit of happiness. In the early 1900s the blueprint for a better life was greatly accepted and easy to process; however, achieving these wanted states of mind left many people a little spiritually bankrupt. Suffice to say, the prosperity consciousness movement à la Quimby had become tainted by people's need for material gain instead of its original curative path which was to understand the riches of the universe. Knowledge of the divine principle meant you could align yourself with spiritual awareness, although it was soon discovered that it also provided keys to acquire fame and fortune. Many people applied the rules set by *The Master Key System* and New Thought movement that transformed doubtful thinking into the wealthiest of lifestyles and proved to be successful. Having said this, we have to ask ourselves the question which seems to pervade authentic power: Is there a blueprint for getting rich?

There have been numerous books devoted to acquiring financial wealth and abundance such as *Think and Grow Rich* by Napoleon Hill (1883) and Dale Carnegie's *How to Win Friends and Influence People* (1936). Books like these augmented internal questioning of how and why this information had been previously kept from the general public. The teachings of the New Thought movement taught how to look inside yourself and allowed the believer to have total control of their life in order to achieve whatever lifestyle was desired. This poses the question that if all we had to do to live a more prosperous life was to look internally at ourselves, then who were the ones who taught us that we need external salvation in the first place?

I am so grateful that my research guided me to study the most notable of scholars in the world of prosperity consciousness. Their anecdotes, outlook and contributions have made me omnivorous in doing this mental excavation. Since studying the powerful teachings of the New Thought movement, I have been led to even further, deeper levels of enlightenment. I cite the New Thought movement as a cornerstone in human development which has influenced many people even to this day. The movement sought to inspire people to acquire the life they desired by understanding ancient wisdom. There is one person, however, that epitomized ancient thought and pioneered within the movement, reaching unprecedented levels. Her contribution and insight was second to none and that person was Emma Curtis Hopkins.

Emma was considered to be a key figure in the New Thought movement and she also pioneered changing the roles of women in the church. Many women went on to form their own versions of churches inspired by her teachings. Emma Hopkins wrote many books on mysticism, metaphysics and Scientific Christian mental practices. She was once quoted as saying, "My judgment is right judgment, as I judge, so it is." This was straight out of ancient concepts as she also went on to say, "All the poise that I AM I radiate through all the universe and all things feel the joy of adjustment." Her approach was primarily spiritual in the sense that before it was named anything else, it was natural thinking and universal understanding rather than a religious doctrine. Here is an excerpt of her powerful teachings about how to see your own brilliance. This is taken from her writings entitled *The Radiant I Am.*

"It is the teaching that all is Spirit, and matter is not obedient shadow-picturing thereof, which is the final subtle message toward me that makes me see that I AM what I AM and alter not. Spirit is the gentle Mother doctrine among the doctrines of the world – gentle but inexorable. She brings to exposure the Man Child, my I AM – who

shall rule all nations with a rod of iron. The iron that is strongest is magnetic. It rules in the earth by holding all the particles together. It rules in the sun. It rules in all the spheres. They roll because of the magnet. So all my being has moved because of my I AM. So all my universe shall wheel to my ordination.

This is my ministry. I am glad to give myself to my Self and to give all my world to my Self and let my Self do in judgment twelve works upon the earth.

This is my ministry. I have heard all I shall ever hear. I know all I shall ever know. I now make my Self known.

I make my Self known by speaking, thinking, writing and living the word of my Self – my I AM."

Emma Curtis Hopkins

As I read the works of many scholars I always tend to go digging afterwards because there is so much dissension and avarice when it comes to knowledge. When I go digging I wonder why we all can't go to the well of abundant knowing, grab a spoon and help ourselves to this awareness. There are so many versions and interpretations of knowledge that we have to decide how big a spoon we actually need to scoop it all. In my case my eyes are clearly bigger than my stomach because while reading Emma Hopkins, I did what I always do, only this time I didn't grab a spoon, I needed a shovel to plow through the depths of where I was being taken. The wealth of knowledge that Miss Hopkins was sharing found me, to my delight, arriving at the doors of Ancient Egypt, begging to be let in to dig for more treasures of spiritual awakening.

Meet the Fillmores

If we want an example of New Thought validation on how the universe works, let us see the example from Charles and Myrtle Fillmore. Charles Fillmore (1854-1948) was a prosperous man although he came from humble beginnings. When he and his wife Myrtle were struggling financially, they moved to Kansas City where a friend recommended they attend the lectures of Dr. E. B. Weeks, whom Emma Hopkins had sent there to teach. Charles didn't find anything useful within the lessons outlined by Mr. Weeks or his message, however Myrtle had a revelation.

Myrtle Fillmore (1845-1931) was a college-educated woman and came from a family with a history of tuberculosis. She was well read and opinionated until the family illness struck and she was weakened by its symptoms. The Fillmores tried all kinds of remedial practices to cure tuberculosis although nothing seemed to work. With the economic downturn affecting their finances, this also served to frustrate their housing situation. During the lecture from Dr. Weeks, Myrtle was inspired by a sentence that, as she put it, "turned her life around." She said, referring to her illness, "I am a child of God, and therefore I do not inherit sickness." This productive thinking put the healing process in motion. Although it took nearly two years of constant affirmations, Myrtle in fact did get better from that moment. Something miraculous had happened; she was a changed person and people around her wanted to know what she had done that made the difference.

Charles was apparently so impressed by her recovery that he began to study world practices of philosophy and taught the links between religion and science. They both shared their principles with students and others began to experience their own healings as a result. In a matter of months, Myrtle had established a reputation in the area as a healer and teacher, and set up what is known today as the Unity School of Christianity. The teachings of the Fillmores were mostly metaphysical, and in time they actually went to Chicago to study with Emma Hopkins herself.

The Fillmores had created such a high profile of themselves in the world of prosperity conscious movement that they went on to publish a magazine in 1889, and named the movement Unity in 1891. Even to this day The Unity Church is the largest New Thought movement with in excess of over 75,000 members.

> ## "All causes are essentially mental, and whosoever comes into daily contact with a high order of thinking must take on some of it."

Charles Fillmore

The above quote from Charles is profoundly seated in the laws of the universe. Do you recognize the echoing of the Law of Attraction? This formula was used long before the movie *The Secret* glorified this precept.

The fundamental beliefs in New Thought are:

▲ *The Divine is in all things.*

▲ *The mind is much more real and powerful than matter.*

The new consciousness paradigm suggests many ways to achieve prosperity. You are encouraged to take the knowledge of other prosperous people and find your own way of achieving your goals. The New Thought movement set a blueprint for success and, that being said, let me answer the question which I seem to be avoiding, and I do so because the answer is simple, too simple in fact for some people. Is there a blueprint for getting rich? The answer is an emphatic... Yes.

The Six Views of
Seeing Sense

What You See is What You Get
Settle This!
Subjective Perspective

PART TWO:
They Came, They Saw, They Conquered

Chapter 5:

The Six Views
of Seeing Sense

In previous chapters we looked at the historical views exemplified by the leaders who started the New Thought movement. It is a great field of study and liberating to know that many pioneers developed the ancient laws of prosperous thinking into a new movement. However, in searching for the alleged beginning, the origins of New Thought are shrouded in mystery and the reason for this misdirection is that there isn't really a beginning to speak of. The key to understanding the principles of ancient knowledge lay in its spheres of consciousness that are always evolving. Consciousness eclipses itself over many time periods and when we are ready to use this knowledge, only then can we enroll in the universal celestial classroom.

"When the student is ready the
master teacher will appear."

Ancient proverb

It is wonderful to see how this knowledge has been a major influence in today's society by virtue of self-help gurus and inspirational speakers. These mind-mapping magicians such as Jim Rohn, Anthony Robbins, Les Brown, Dr. Wayne Dwyer, Richard Bandler, to name a few, take the world stage and remind us how to get in touch with ancient principles in order to resolve our own mystery. It is wise to pay homage to these teachings as it gives us a sense of belonging and something to reach for in our own search for identity. In this chapter we will start to explore a deeper significance to the ancient principles of prosperity so that we can arm ourselves with the tools to achieve our own goals.

Before we start using our own view effectively, first we need to decipher what it means to have a "perceptive" mindset and then we can work out the "perspective" in our lives. The word perception comes from the Latin *percipere* which means to obtain or gather. Metaphorically, it also means to grasp with the mind. Perspective, on the other hand, means to look closely at something – *per* meaning through and *specere* meaning to look deeper at something. It also refers to giving the appearance of form or a particular way of viewing things that depends on one's experience and personality; for example, in the illustrative sense of a picture or a drawing that gives the appearance of depth and form.

Everyone should pay more attention to the words perception and perspective as our lives depend on them. Personally, I use these two words before every coaching session with clients to see how I can be of service to their vision. The preliminary stage in a coaching session offers many benefits for revealing how a coach sees the client's surroundings and, more importantly, how the clients see themselves. People use coaching for a variety of reasons in order to receive clarity to their desired outcomes. A better way to understand the difference between these two words is perception relates to the road of how a person thinks and perspective as the visual map of how to reach the desired destination. In fact every therapist, counselor and coach should have these words imbedded in their repertoire.

"There are things known and there are things unknown, and in between are the door of perception."

Aldous Huxley

Humankind has a habit of defining their perspective with the naming of things to correspond with the five senses. Categorizing what we see, hear, touch, taste and smell only serves to discern from other sensations so that we can identify everything. For instance, when you taste or touch something that you don't recognize, the brain automatically relates that information with something that you are familiar with, even if it has a completely new experience of its own. For example, if you taste a new type of meat you might say that it tastes like chicken because of our fundamental gauge of how chicken should taste. Another example is if you touch something and it feels coarse in texture, you might say that it feels tough like leather. Being "like leather" is quickly recognized as a relative image because it's already in our mental filing system. When someone displays a callous or emotionless personality they can be described as being "hard as nails." No one is actually ever "hard as nails" but again by adding perspective we can illustrate and communicate our point with a visual reference.

Prosperous people challenge their view by being creative and pushing their perceptive boundaries. If we rely on being compliant, we stop questioning the world around us and we lose our sense of feeling independent. This compliance affects our perception and if we are not conscious of misdirected filtering, even our taste buds are predetermined, like with the chicken metaphor I used earlier. I mean you wouldn't bite into an apple and expect to taste an orange or an onion would you? But why not? Well, in essence you are responsible for convincing your brain how an apple should taste and you reward your taste buds with that perception even before you take your first bite.

Throughout our lives we are given many rules and boundaries to keep us logical and uniquely diffident. Placing distance between the oligarchy (those who govern our lives) and us naturalistic beings means we can have our own views about the world while co-existing with each other. Simply put, we should listen to our own internal judgment and start new trends of being individual. There are rules to becoming prosperous yet the beauty of achieving it is the knowledge that there is more than one way to create enlightenment. Let us define the difference between prosperous and successful people to show how results are achieved by minor shifts in mindset.

Successful people embody the very definition of the word success. The etymology of success means "following one thing after another as a continued action." However, this is rather vague as you can also be a success at not being productive. Example: if you are degenerated in your thinking process and think in a degenerated fashion, you could call that a success. If you do something in a haphazard way, especially if you continue to do so, this is also a success. The same is true even if you are inclined to not expect productivity in your life, then this is deemed being successful. I mean to say that's great, because you're achieving what you set out to do.

Prosperous people, on the other hand, are productive whether they succeed or fail at something because they remain victorious with their natural productive trait. The difference is quite eye-opening. Successful people are results driven and accomplished personalities whereas prosperous people are ever flourishing with whatever they attempt. There are similarities between the two mindsets but there are defining clues that expand your pursuit of clearly seeing sense. I have cited these as having six views.

The six views of seeing sense are:

1. Mindset

When you possess the qualities of being prosperous you will have an advantage over linear-minded people. Mindset is the reason prosperity is highly attractive because the linear mind is easily manipulated whereas the prosperous mind is liberated.

2. Visualization

Prosperous people use visualization. They picture in their mind how they expect to achieve results by living as if their goals have already been accomplished. Visualizing your desires is one thing; however, if you do not interact with them by acting, living and breathing as if they are already manifested then your intentions will be lost.

3. Creativity

Mind power interaction is about seeing the unseen and by being creative with what you want. The key here is to do this constantly and think of the outcome you expect. Once you start using your creative side you will notice opportunities all around you that you didn't see before. You should start by living and seizing every opportunity to be creative and become more productive.

4. Process is Contagious

When you surround yourself with people that make things happen, their actions have a good chance of rubbing off on you. Read about entrepreneurial people that have become successful. They follow a process that should motivate, uplift and inspire you to follow suit and will be a good indication of how you should be conducting your own life.

5. Consistency

When you ask your mind to work with you, you illustrate consistency. Being focused and determined means you are keeping the ambitions alive and ever flowing.

6. Preparation

Preparation is a key component for using your mind to attract what you entertain. The achievement of prosperity starts by you making room in your life by preparing it in this dimension. Start today by preparing the way for everything desired. For example, you could wear certain clothes that emulate the position of someone you admire for a desired lifestyle to be achieved.

When you adopt the identity of that which you want to portray, you begin to rewrite your own rules of being. Be the author of your own life and write the next chapter of what you expect. How do you think I wrote this book? First, I sent my script out into the universe to breathe using the six principles above then I entertained that it could be done by visualizing it into existence. You too should begin to listen to your subconscious, and once you stop waiting for something external to happen, the universe will indicate that prosperity is something you always had access to without your knowing it. I don't want to sound too much like The Secret by promoting the Law of Attraction because the source of this knowing is more than thinking positive. There is an all too common illusion that if you think of failure you will create more of it in your life. There is evidence that that can happen – however, consider this:

> ## "Prosperous thinking welcomes failure because it is how we learn that something doesn't work."

> ### Rico Griffiths-Taitte

In other words, **use failure to learn from undesirable outtakes**.

Productive thinking instructs you use all of your senses to see your outcomes. When you start thinking in this way you will wonder how you managed to be so blind for so long. Prosperous people adopt the following blueprint for achievement:

▲ *They are solution focused and they learn from experience.*

▲ *They create their own success while others wait for success to create them.*

▲ *They are motivated by fear.*

▲ *They are inquisitive which makes them perfect researchers.*

▲ *They take responsibility for their actions and outcomes.*

▲ *Prosperous people use their time wisely. They are constantly planning, writing and preparing to get things done.*

▲ *They are ambitious and they don't associate with toxic people.*

▲ *They are students first and experts second.*

▲ *They are completely focused and deal with challenges effectively.*

▲ *They constantly find ways to improve themselves and are inspired by change.*

▲ *Prosperous people make results-based decisions.*

▲ *They process that the universe seeks balance and learn quickly to adapt to every situation.*

▲ *Prosperous people meander in different forms to flow in, out and through any situation.*

▲ *They are strong-minded in knowing they could lose everything tomorrow, but as long as they have breath, they can breathe life into another opportunity.*

▲ *They are resilient and adaptable to embrace change.*

▲ *They set higher standards for themselves.*

▲ *Prosperous people work, they do not have jobs. A job is something you do. Working is something you love doing.*

Understanding these rules, or at the very least attempting to emulate them, will propel you to be in total control of your destiny. Write out this list and go over these traits whenever you need inspiration. Read them while on your way to work. Try to memorize some of them and, most of all, live by them. Write some of your own by adding to the list.

What You See is What You Get

We are the source of everything that we entertain and knowing this means we can redefine our existence to our advantage and then our prosperity will be granted. We should use our own internal judgment and create new ways to change the way we look at things. When we become creative we can choose whether or not to stay in situations that make us feel uncomfortable and expand our options. There are rules to becoming prosperous and one of these rules states that there are many ways to create the life you desire. That desire starts by forgiving those moments when we entertain non-productive thought patterns. We have the ability to reform and shape those patterns from cocooned ignorance into the emergent butterfly we aspire to be.

We see far more than we give ourselves credit for and we should be aware of who we are and what we represent. This will begin to manifest when we listen to our internal guidance, otherwise known as intuition. Intuition is an important word because inside the meaning and the spelling of the word denotes the lesson of our own being. Let's break this down:

In-tuition: in = being, tuition = schooling.

Being in school, you are a pupil and as a pupil you are like the pupil of your eye or window to your soul. Our higher intellect and third eye is also known as our mind's eye. In fact it isn't our actual eyes that see at all but the whole body that sees through the senses. We are sensory beings, or at least we should be, and there is no better example of us being sensory than when we were infants. It is in these early stages of development that we were much more than just sensory; we are elementals. The body vessel in which we arrive at this earthly plane has all the coordinates of nature because we bring with us an abundant knowledge of earth, air, fire and water. These base elements form our molecular structure and naturally align with our universal energy and senses. This energy that we are born with is highly intelligent and intuitive and our only mission in life is to return to the source of that knowledge. What we experience internally and externally during our sojourn here on Earth is a result of patterns and adaptations learned since childhood. We then take these lessons into adulthood and entertain them as real. However, if we remind ourselves how Anton Mesmer introduced ancient techniques of mind cure to the masses, he was vilified for thinking differently. Thinking and acting differently illustrates a fear in mainstream society, which is ironic, as people constantly search for their own identity. There is a seeming contradiction here as we humans strive to be individual while also craving acceptance. Striving for acceptance comes from the ego and what that means is so much of what we learned as elementals is lost as we grow into the known world, but what about the unknown world? For some people, this a scary thought. The unknown seems like an existence where there are no rules, no here or there, no this thing or that thing. The masters of ancient thought called this existence Enlightenment.

Our opinions are hitherto measured by the imprints of our parents and the blueprints of our puppet-masters. What we don't do enough of is trust our birthright instincts to lead the way and make decisions based on our individual findings. All said and done, it seems to make perfect sense not to question what is right in front of you, doesn't it? If the general consensus agrees unanimously, how dare we be different and question the masses? However, isn't everything questionable? There should be healthy skepticism about everything. The phrase "ignorance is bliss for it is folly to be wise" is a great example of the word compliance, but even compliance refers to us not doing our own homework. A better description for going with the flow is the word settling.

Settle This!

Many of us have heard teachers in classrooms say, "Okay, now children, settle down." We are even groomed by this word in our professional careers and lifestyle. Shall I remind you of the advice your guardians gave you? "When you leave school you should get a good job and settle down." Same is true for finding a life partner. We hear from our friends and parents: "Isn't it time you settled down?" Even in conflicting relationships when those around us predicted the outcome and warned us to take heed, did we listen? No, thus we "settled". The way we all look at life is unquestionably similar and provokes much intrigue to an analytical mind. Yes it is true that we settle into situations that make us feel comfortable but this view is usually the result of what we are exposed to emotionally. When we look metaphysically at the word "emotion" we get E = energy + motion, in other words, it's our feelings that make us react.

The connotation of the word "information" means that we can amiably break down this word from a metaphysical standpoint. The original vernacular for the meaning of the word information was "light code." For example, it is said that if you tell someone something, you are "in-forming" that person. I stated earlier that this was "light coded" and once that person knew more information about something they became enlightened on the subject. This information is prevalent when we communicate with others using varying degrees of adaptations to express ourselves physically or verbally. Our tone of voice, pitch, and sensations all contribute to

79

emotionally telegraph our message. In doing so, we also need to add the word "meaning" to our message if we want the recipient to converse on the same level of understanding. Let me explain. When someone tells us something they usually strive for perspective to validate their statements by asking, "Do you know what I mean?" as if to say, "Do you see things as I see them?" or "Am I making myself clear?" Another example is "Do you see what I'm saying?" quite blatantly using perspective as a reference of agreement.

The inquisitive ones among us are curious to find out who or what implanted these metaphoric references, comparing one thing to another in the first place. Asking these kinds of questions not only separate you from the norm, whatever "the norm" is; it also allows you to be open-minded encouraging you to form your own opinion about everything. The benefits of asking yourself these types of questions and seeing things in this way liberates you from accepting that which has been presented in front of you. Generally speaking, society expects us to be compliant with our views, although this is not how prosperous goal-oriented people see. Ironically we rarely hear people say what they mean or mean what they say, hence why they end their statements with furtive questioning. This is not a character flaw, as we humans only know the world by virtue of how we communicate through our meaning of sight, sound, touch, taste and smell. However, it was the German scientist Edmund Husserl who said, "Meaning is the intention of the mind"; he was referring to the mind's eye, meaning our perspective view.

Subjective Perspective

Our views hold no official knowing on what is true until we create a logical reason that makes sense to us. This is well played out during a Rorschach test, or more commonly known as an inkblot test. When a client has an inkblot in front of them the analyst may ask a simple question like, "What do you see in this image?" The client's answer will be the dialectic exchange of how they engage shape and form. For example, have you ever looked up at the sky and seen the shape of faces or animals in the clouds? You may have seen a significant image in a splash of liquid on a surface. What you are seeing is nature's inkblot test where our eyes construct details that may not necessarily exist yet playfully we entertain what could be.

Coaching is never a subjective experience on the part of the coach. No therapist, counselor or life coach would attempt self-help applications without first relating to their client, or building rapport with them. They refrain from any personal opinion, only constructing their client's perspective. Is your linear thinking hurting yet? Don't worry; it gets easier to understand once you use your creativity and not logic to unleash spiritual liberty. However, before we leave this chapter on perception, we can't really talk about perception without somehow mentioning Maurice Merleau-Ponty's work. I am an avid fan of Merleau-Ponty and in my early thirties I read a book that he wrote called *The Phenomenology of Perception* which altered my view on perception as a theoretical study. Merleau-Ponty, for me at least, set new horizons on how our visual acceptance shapes how we govern our lives. How we think we are supposed to act is tainted by an illusion. That illusion relies on our sedentary mindset in an effort to confuse our own judgment on how to behave. Below is an excerpt of Merleau-Ponty's view:

"I cannot shut myself up within the realm of science. All my knowledge of the world, even my scientific knowledge, is gained from my own particular point of view, or from some experience of the world without which the symbols of science would be meaningless..."

He then went on to say:

"I am not a 'living creature' nor even a 'man', nor again even 'a consciousness' endowed with all the characteristics which zoology, social

anatomy or inductive psychology recognize in these various products of the natural or historical process — I am the absolute source, my existence does not stem from my antecedents, from my physical and social environment; instead it moves out toward them and sustains them, for I alone bring into being for myself."

We could sit all day trying to postulate whether thinking positive actually works, which really shouldn't be our main objective. What is interesting about Merleau-Ponty's observation is that it is not pompous to question everything; it just enforces our investigative ability to be erudite.

As we migrate from the beginnings of the New Thought movement it is easy for us to take the visual high ground set by ancient leaders because they no longer entertain our physical realm. However, we should respect their guidance as they paved the way for us to profit from being spiritually connected. What should not be dismissed however is how the universe delivers its promise to profit from seeking a unique outlook. We should start being proactive and meet our expectations halfway by altering our perspective. Start challenging your regimented lifestyle. Continue to push the limitations you place upon yourself and accept no less than what you expect to achieve. We will discover how to do this in later chapters but, for now, entertain that the universe has no other choice but to mirror your understanding of who you are. As soon as you start thinking about the universe's core principles, what you think you are will be revealed in your actions.

"Whether you think you can or you think you can't, you're right."

Henry Ford

Eye of the Storm

PART TWO:
They Came, They Saw, They Conquered

Chapter 6:

Eye of the Storm

Hurricanes and tornadoes are forces of nature that cause devastation everywhere they go. They are developed from thunderstorms and extend from clouds that swirl around in a rotating column of air and can travel along land or sea. These thunderstorms generate strong winds and debris as they move along their path. Scientists and storm chasers alike are both intrigued and in awe about how these phenomena create such turbulent energies. Although they are destructive, ironically at the center of these hurricanes it is usually calm and known as the eye of the storm. By all accounts the center is clear in comparison to the devastation that surrounds it. The energy produced at this epicenter generates heat and has very little cloud or destruction. Hurricanes and tornadoes leave nothing standing in their path and can render a town or city immobile, leaving it in a state of carnage and the aftermath can leave people's lives totally shattered.

I started this chapter with the description of hurricanes and tornadoes because I wanted to address our perception of fear and loss. Losing someone or something you love deeply can turn your world upside down and can be very painful indeed. Loss includes a whirlwind of emotions like sadness and confusion, and we can also experience devastation just like a tornado. There are occasions when we do not find the answers to comfort us in our times of loss or in a rejected state. For example, a conflicting relationship or the rejection from a desired job can lead to feelings of abandonment and possibly trauma. Somewhere in our internal knowing we must accept that feeling this way is a normal reaction even though our emotions are whirling around in disbelief. It may be difficult to communicate exactly how we feel during this time, but allowing ourselves to be hurt is part of the healing process. We are advised that time heals all ails and while this may be true we must placate ourselves knowing that there is no right or wrong way to grieve.

Grieving is a very individual thing, yet there are healthy ways to assist in restoring our perception of any tragic occurrence. I mention this because I too identified with the pernicious state of loss when I received the news about my eye. I felt that I had lost the very thing I needed to be an artist. I had totally lost the use of my left eye, and the trauma that we talked about earlier is such a powerful emotion in all of us that it can be soul-destroying, especially when we lose sight of ourselves. It comforted me to discover that even ancient enlightened masters occasionally felt pain. Their mastery lay in knowing how to deflect the energy of any painful experience within their own being. Some masters resolved painful occurrences through meditation, because they knew that allowing the stillness of the mind could overcome physical feelings. It is this stillness referred to as "still point" that causes everything to clear away not just some, but all impurities that taint our physical and emotional state. The best way to achieve this form of clarity is acknowledging that we humans are in no way perfect, nor should we try to be. There are obviously going to be rough times in life, but it is the pursuit of perfection that we should concentrate on and not perfection itself.

It is often necessary for the metaphoric tornado within us all to destroy unwanted behaviors around us, just so we can start afresh.

We need clarity both mentally and spiritually, and Just like the eye of the storm it is our own central tunnel of light that creates new beginnings to deal with the torrent of life. We all have suffered loss of some kind at one time or another, leaving us in despair; however, I first want to state that while we are talking about loss, I am not just talking about death. There is a great deal of misunderstanding about our untimely passing as we can only really die once, but there are many variations of loss. When we struggle with a problem or an answer to something we often feel as if the issue should be resolved quickly. We seem to forget that we are the embodiment of pressure and born into a world of intention. The word intention means to stretch and we should give ourselves a round of applause for the amount of stretching we have to do in life. We can relate this to the hurricane and tornado metaphor where everything around us is seemingly destructive and full of emotional debris. When we look through the eyes of prosperity we learn that the universe has at times a sacrificial price in seeking enlightenment and presents a toll that needs to be paid. This is not something to be fearful of, just observe that when we focus on the life or goal that we desire, we first have to decide how much of ourselves we can afford to devote to those desires. Like I said, this can at times come at a painful sacrificial price just so we learn from the process. The toll of these emotions inhibits many people from even chasing their goals, dreams and aspirations out of fear.

The Perception of Fear

One of the most world renowned and often misunderstood powers known to the human mind is fear. By its very nature fear is a vital response to the physical and emotional threat we feel daily. For example, some people have a fear of small spaces (claustrophobia) and some have a fear of flying (aerophobia) etc. There are as many types of fears as there are names for everything on this earth. Our social climate is preoccupied with fear; for example, some may fear going to work for whatever reason but there is a global fear that if we don't go to our respective jobs, we can't maintain our responsibilities. It is this fear of losing our livelihoods that is the driving force that motivates us to carry on. The panic of keeping or securing our jobs is ironic when there is no such thing as job security anymore. We are frightened of being socially deprived yet we expect to live well above our basic needs. I said earlier in this book that our core values have changed and it seems that fear, panic, jealousy, envy and doubt are varying degrees of the same social fear.

The only thing we seem to afford with our fears is the cost of our morality. For example, we put on a brave face when we are in situations that make us feel uncomfortable. To really see what fear is and to understand it means anything that slightly reminds us of a traumatic possibility makes us cautious and defensive resulting in a "fight or flight" response. As I said earlier, ironically this keeps us in check, because if we didn't feel this fear we couldn't protect ourselves from the very thing that frightens us. When we are scared or frightened it shows in our physical body as an innate response for coping with danger. This is so evident that when we fear something, our heart rate is accelerated, the blood vessels dilate and we have increased muscle tension and breathing rate. After a series of physiological changes, only then does our subconscious realize the emotion of fear. There is another emotion with the same symptoms as described above. It has the same adrenalin rush and experience of anxiety and is called ecstasy, otherwise known as the heightened state of happiness. This means that fear is so powerful and so personal that not only are we scared of fear but also in awe of it.

In my own personal battle with fear I have come to realize that it was my lack of confidence in my abilities which elicited random thoughts of being afraid. I have had many conflicting moments with the fear of failing, which is common, but the effects of this can cripple even the most confident person. This fear of failing goes against everything I stand for now, but when I began my journey of how prosperous people lived, I learned very quickly about the beauty of allowing myself to make mistakes. I also learned how to free-fall into greatness and the lesson here is that too often we tend to allow fear to have dominion over us. We subconsciously give our authentic power away, which ultimately leaves us open to being spiritually and emotionally attacked. Let's look at this definition of the word fear:

A feeling of agitation and anxiety caused by the presence or imminence of danger.

Fear also means:

Extreme reverence or awe toward a supreme power.

Fear Busting

If there is a continual threat of something to be afraid of, we can find ourselves forever in a state of protecting our neuroses. There are so many things that could frighten us during our lives that we should applaud the fact that we make it through the day. The key word here is survival and when we survive any probable threat posed to us, it shows that we are actually capable of overcoming adversities and being more productive rather than focusing on things to be scared of. Having said this, when we feel that something threatens us how do we overcome fear? How do we embrace it? Can fear be used in a productive way to defeat itself?

In Chapter 2 I mentioned that seminal movie *The Matrix* where in the last battle scene we are given a front row seat educating us on what it takes to overcome anything we are conflicted about. The main character Neo, while in battle with Agent Smith and Co, finds enlightenment via the premise of letting go all that he fears. This brilliant lesson in "enlightenment 101" teaches us that Neo not only realizes his power from within, but also that he didn't need anything external of himself to see there was no threat in the first place. The penultimate victory was achieved when he used this knowledge to defeat his nemesis by rendering himself as one of them. How Neo achieved this will be discussed in later chapters; however, we must come to realize that our illusion of despair serves to paralyze any physical or mental endurance. Learning to let go of these illusions teaches us how to control fear and consume it, to understand fear and overcome it. The phrase "There is nothing to fear but fear itself" is quite useful here, and although we are talking about prosperity, it is crucial to mention that people who fear making decisions or find it difficult to focus find themselves in a permissive state of giving in to fear of the unknown.

I See Dread People

Some of the clients that I coach who suffer from this type of fear were easy for me to identify when I met them for their first session. I could immediately see that these people lived in the same area geographically. I could even name their native country in an instant as they each share the same fear-based patterns. The name of that country is that over-populated nation of sufferers who deteriorate on mass from the same anxiety. You might be able to recognize the people I'm referring to. They live in the land called "What if." You see, fear and doubt go everywhere together and the climate in the land of "What if" has very cloudy skies making it difficult to see clearly. It's almost impossible to breathe anywhere in the land of "What if" because the air is so dense. The people from this land always travel together and they need lots of hands to carry all that baggage on their journeys, called the "What if journeys." These journeys have no real destination and totally unexpected outcomes. This scares them into bringing every single item along with them. Their most common trait is that they are all related to one another. Their last name is Case and their first names are either Justine or Justin. Oh yes! The people of "What if" are prepared for their travels but because they are always frightened, the Case families end up not going anywhere at all, just in case. Look, I'm making light of this subject but I would never trivialize the good town folk of "What if." Their state of mind is important and in no way would I try to sound apathetic – anyway I couldn't, I have respect for the dread!

There is a state of mind that anyone seeking a life of prosperity will need to grasp to overcome fear-based patterns and fully comprehend the power of the universe. This fear factor seems to have been initiated in our childhood, making us aware of the dangers of uncertainty, making it harder to form an identity. Our own belief system and faith may have been suggested early in our nurturing because of the fear of us leading into a transient state of nothingness. Spiritual gurus could challenge that there's nothing wrong with this; however, it is very rare in western culture that we should become detached from the spoils of this world and seek pure nothingness.

Understanding this nothingness starts with us knowing that we are the sole beneficiaries to prosperity consciousness. It is our birthright to be prosperous, in fact the universe wants nothing more for us than to realize the abyss of abundant offerings we have at our disposal. We seem to lose sight of our birthright to be happy now and in every moment. We can prepare for everything in life except one eventuality and that is death. Oh sure, we can make funeral arrangements before we die but the actual transition is untimely. As I said, we seek to be prepared for everything as the need for preparation seems to rule our existence, even in our childhood.

Question: What do we call the private education in England where children go from the ages of eight to 13? That's right, a preparatory school. We are told to go to school, get a good education, get a good job, or else! We are trained to live in fear of not being prepared instead of being guided to be brilliant. That's what differs from the ancient mind paradigm and the vaunted lifestyle of today's youth: the lack of sufficient guidance to be magnificent.

Courage

In 1952 the American philosopher Paul Tillich wrote a book called *The Courage To Be* in which he referred to the realization that most of us suffer from an unpredictable existence which has no real purpose. Tillich is absolutely correct, not just with an analytical mind, but a metaphysical one. He suggests that we come into being at birth and then learn about life solely through our daily experiences. He goes on to say that there is no tangible, absolute or resolute notion that many of us have a real purpose. What Tillich endorses in *The Courage To Be* is that to have courage means to have strength to continue to live on in a meaningful way, despite the fact that our existence appears to have no purpose at all. Fear, doubt, despair, the ego, hate and self-loathing are an ever present danger that we have to relinquish in order to benefit from "non-being," otherwise known as being enlightened.

Anyone who has ever been on the path of enlightenment is expected to have an understanding that man's greatest fear is thinking that he is alone. This does not concern seekers of the truth because to the spiritually aware attachment is frowned upon. There is a great divide between the material world and the state of "non-being." I would like to point out that I am in no way imposing my own personal views about the validity of your own belief system, I am merely bringing to the table of enlightenment how other people achieved prosperity. Let us recognize that the ethics of nothingness is the quintessential ingredient for knowledge of abundance. When we fall victim to any addiction or attachment, we separate ourselves from the path of being focused, which is corrosive and causes physical and mental illness. In fact fearful or anxious people suffer greatly from this detached persona thus turning to such addictions as alcoholism and drugs just to be able to feel alive. Courage is the fundamental acceptance of having a relationship with the divine principle of being spiritually aware. Our faith in that awareness infinitely transcends our connection to universal power. I highly recommend a further in-depth study of the book *The Courage To Be* because at its fundamental level it is reminiscent of every prosperity manual needed to lead to a path of a meaningful existence.

> "Courage is resistance to fear,
> mastery of fear, not absence of fear."

Mark Twain

Look the Part

We have seen that we are all shaped by our urges, anxieties, fears and idiosyncratic gestures that affirm our identity. Our motives and behaviors are well planned subconsciously from infancy. How we exhibit those behaviors is what we should question, beginning with our thinking pattern. I am an advocate of the New Thought movement and its holistic teachings. After years of researching how ancient thought has been changed to suit a particular time period, I was introduced to Neuro-Linguistic Programing. This new way of thinking, shortened to the better known acronym NLP, was a natural migration for me into the perception of the human mind. What NLP does is combust our human excuses of unwanted states and replaces them with more productive outcomes.

NLP examines the process of finding common traits in our personalities, calling them patterns. These patterns tell us how effectively we process information according to our own perspective. In ancient times, unlocking the secrets to these traits was revealed to the chosen few. Now we have resuscitated this ancient study of the mind because of our modern thirst for knowledge. Through NLP we are asking more interesting questions than ever before about how to enrich our lives and how to liberate our minds. One of the presuppositions in NLP states: "People make the best choices available to them at the time." This is a unique observation as people act and react based on what they decide is right for them at any given moment. But isn't this what Paul Tillich was suggesting many years before NLP came about? How can we act in any other way other than with what we have been taught? Right! Yes indeed, I welcome NLP because of its one-stop-shop approach to dealing with human perception and scrutiny of the mind.

When we see the definition of what it means to have a personality, we learn that it just describes a "mask", or a human being, but a human, being what? The word "character" has its original definition as a symbol or imprint on the soul, being of a defining quality. All this is quite poetic in a nondescript way of describing who or what we are at any one time. If this is true about our physical self, then what about the soul? Let's look at the definition:

Soul: The spirit or immaterial part of a person, the seat of human personality, intellect, will and emotions. It is regarded as an entity that survives the body even after death.

Okay, I have three questions for you:

▲ *What happens when the personality and the soul don't match?*

▲ *Does the soul know itself irrespective of who we think we are?*

▲ *Do our bodies conflict with our higher self?*

The answers to the questions above, or at least part of the answers, can be found in Chapter 10, Seeing the Light. The other answers are for you to decide because only you know. A good place to start is by standing in front of a mirror and taking a good long look at yourself. Start by dismissing what you look like physically and ask the questions above again. Do you really know every facet about who you are compared to how others see you?

People are in search of enriching their lives and liberating their minds, as I stated earlier, and in order to create a harmonious mind, body and spirit we must be aware of the circle of influence we create. These circles, otherwise known as friends or relationships, are very telling in shaping our environment. The path taken by prosperous people selects their circle very carefully as other people's intentions and personalities can serve to either help or hinder us in our search for our goals and desires. When you are ready to walk a different path from those with ulterior energy to your own, your awareness will become heightened and more sensitive. The footprints of your past and the road you have traveled will disappear from view as your new path shines a light to the destination of your desires.

Alice:	*"Oh, no, no. I was just wondering if you could help me find my way."*
Cheshire Cat:	*"Well that depends on where you want to get to."*
Alice:	*"Oh, it really doesn't matter, as long as..."*
Cheshire Cat:	*"Then it really doesn't matter which way you go."*

The above scene is from *Alice in Wonderland* which is one of my all-time favorite movies. It is riddled with examples of how we perceive our journey in life, highlighting our own limitations that we place upon ourselves. Our goals, dreams and ambitions can feel a lot like Alice who was trying desperately to find her way home. The people, places and events that were presented to Alice (or even Dorothy in *The Wizard of Oz* for that matter) shaped their circle of influence. We too have to decide if those around us will lead us off our chosen path. It's worth acknowledging that other people's actions are mostly tolerable, although human behavioral patterns dictate repetition in their endeavors. When seeking enlightenment, other people's deeds will sooner or later reveal their true nature. I'm not suggesting that you will lose friends on the path of enlightenment, but you will gain insight to your goals in search of a more prosperous circle of influence. In essence you will attract those that will be conducive to your development instead of condemning it.

People may start seeing you as different and even become jealous of your achievements to better yourself. Ironically, in society being different results in public scrutiny which is part of the reward for becoming a unique individual. Prosperous people do not focus on whether they are accepted or not because their mindset adopts the state of being liberated. When they use their spiritual fortitude to advance in society they forge ahead without fear of unpopularity. When we are fearless it is then that we affiliate with who we are naturally, especially in relationships.

The Look of Love

I mentioned at the beginning of this chapter about loss and feeling devastated by using the analogy of hurricanes and tornados. I also mentioned that we could lose sight of ourselves, which is sometimes necessary to clear the debris from our lives, remember! The same is true in bad relationships. Have you ever been in a relationship where the advice from your trusted friends tells you that you shouldn't be with your chosen partner? You are the one involved which means you can't see what others see from the outside looking in, and yet only after the relationship is over do we achieve clarity of who we were inside our partner's influence.

> "Self-knowledge can be obtained only by looking into the mind and virtue of the soul, which is the diviner part of a man, as we see our own image in another's eye."

Plato

When we talk about love in the visionary sense we search for clues whether our senses have tiptoed into the ineffable realm of delight, or that we should get our eyes tested. For example, when we look at the phrase "beauty is in the eye of the beholder" it means that beauty is subjective, unique and individual. Picture the scene: a lady is walking down a busy street in the middle of summer, gracefully parading like a gazelle down a catwalk runway. She is stunningly attractive and knows that everybody is admiring her for her divine essence, the epitome of grace, sophistication and muse. Then you pan down and see this gimp of a man, troll-like in his stature, waddling beside her, hand in hand, knowing what everyone else is thinking. I mean, let's be honest, when we see a beautiful woman with an unattractive man walking down the street, many questions come to mind like: What does she see in him? While others may be thinking: He must be rich or: She should have gone to Specsavers (the optometrist).

There seems to be a perspective paradox on the subject of love. While many of us seek the unconditional kind, this tells us that we want something with much more significance to it, which really can't be described. However, if we return to our beautiful woman and unattractive man scenario and use the adage "the eyes have it" as an example, then is it simply enough to say that we know for sure what beauty is? I hear a unanimous "No."

Indeed, love is blind at the best of times, and the perspective of relationships is one that baffles even the most brilliant of minds. In ancient traditions relationships were never taken for granted, in fact they were revered. The union of man and woman was more retrospective and honored than it is in our modern society. In ancient times sex was a transmutable act reserved solely for the divine principle of procreation. But then something heinous happened. In Victorian times, for example, open discussions of sex were frowned upon because they had a prudish perspective in mainstream society. In fact the subject of human affection was rarely displayed at all and you were held in contempt if your image advertised it. In Victorian times it was not the proper way to express oneself as a sexual deviant. Feeling sexy was an insult to any lady of the day. However, in our modern society there is an obvious aggrandizement of coquettish foreplay in even the most innocent of TV commercials. So what happened to our liberal sense of being in love or appreciation for relationships? The innuendo of the human form is far sexier than the actual act of sex itself. Courtship and wooing of the opposite sex is very reminiscent of the animal magnetism as explored by Franz Anton Mesmer. Slightly revealing a bodily part is far more suggestive and excites the senses much more than the naked form itself. This sexual suggestion in movies and the arts made the British *Curry On* movies for example the roaring success that they were. Innuendo is unfolding the gift of carnal desire, the first proverbial tease, and it suggests that the promise of the prize is more rewarding than the prize itself.

I know I'm digressing off the topic of loss, but the method in my madness shows how the correlation between hurricanes and our personal feelings is also present in the way we relate to other people, especially while in the throes of love. The dynamic between love and hate shows that there is a thin line between them (hmmm, there's a song in there somewhere). I just want to clarify that I'm a great believer of love and an advocate of the unconditional kind. However, love needs to be a two-way exchange and a union of minds. All too often we see the word love used in such a matter of fact way without true displays of respect. The cooing of lovers is without precedence if displays of affection are not echoed with action. Remember the phrase "actions speak louder than words." We must acknowledge that we should love ourselves first unequivocally before attempting to love someone else.

Some people are attracted to conflicting relationships and we should avoid convincing ourselves that feeling hurt in this way is normal. If we are not in tune with the kind of love we want reciprocated, we can experience our internal dialogue to keep replaying those disappointments. In my quest to see love from the perspective of our feelings, I hope I have justified the need to view our potential mates as we see ourselves, which should be a reflection of our own image. The point here is that no matter what situation we are going through, if we choose to stay in the painful experience we will have done a great job of convincing ourselves that pain is the end result of despair. No one should tell you not to be prepared but we should make a valiant effort to migrate from constantly feeling emotional pain. Acknowledgment that we can elevate ourselves from painful ashes makes us proactive instead of reactive. By changing our outlook, prosperity consciousness can teach us how we can be victorious with every decision. This is probably why people use the term "baby steps" when talking about being cautious. Not because we need to slow things down in order to teach us how to achieve something but with baby steps equating to baby knowledge and baby movement, nothing is over processed, over analyzed or over thought. Babies deal with things in a non-sequential, non-committed way thus letting things happen naturally. Even in a new relationship it is advisable to take things slowly and let things develop at their own pace. If we are capable of changing our reactions of being hurt, we can redefine our understanding of feeling loss and embrace the authentic knowing of being comforted, just like a baby.

The Emerald Vision

Personal Transformation
Eye Spy!
Positive and Negative Definition

PART TWO:
They Came, They Saw, They Conquered

Chapter 7:

The Emerald Vision

I identified at the end of the last chapter that we are born with an intelligence which is more advanced than the knowledge we acquire in adulthood. That knowledge was most prominent when we were babies because babies do not judge nor do they know anything other than how to be supreme beings. The mind of a baby processes the world without reason or doubt because they experience things as they are and not via perception. The milieu of a baby's viewpoint doesn't need to qualify its own existence neither does the mind of a child, as their world is very intuitive, creative and full of wonder.

Personal Transformation

When talking about personal transformation, we should acknowledge that our soul's journey is to find our purpose on Earth and learn from the human experience before returning to the light. People who have had near death experiences have reported seeing this light emitting a sense of being welcomed home. They also tell us that this light is filled with pure love and has been referred to by metaphysicians as a "stargate." This stargate has also been described as the porthole of intelligence that assisted us when entering this earthly realm. As we grow from babies into children, the filters in our brains are heavily influenced from our parents' perspective of how to live in a world ruled by the duality of good and bad, night and day, rich and poor etc. When we ourselves become adults we are coerced into a submissive gilded cage of labeling whatever we see unless we decide to make our own judgment. What I mean by this is that our perception is mainly guided by logic instead of how we personally digest the world around us. We are comfortable in dissecting everything in this way and this logic is also known as doing a scientific evaluation. The word science means that a subject is thoroughly investigated, so thorough in fact that our curiosity requires only left-brained thinking. However, in studying ancient transcended states, many gurus and those interested in reaching spiritual awareness enlisted both left-brained and right-brained thinking to view everything as a whole and not as separate events. This ancient thought process was practiced in Predynastic times where our ancient masters called it alchemy.

In my own studies of how the ancients conducted spirituality, I have found many misrepresentations of the uses of alchemy and what it actually means. The general consensus is that alchemy is defined as a practice of transmuting base metals into gold which can produce great riches and therefore even greater universal power. For many centuries, especially in medieval times, alchemists labored over mixing certain base metals like lead and copper to transmute these into gold, which had very little effect. Other literature suggests that there was a way to use alchemy to advance the human potential to higher states of learning. While these schools of thought are not wrong, ancient texts consider the real power of alchemy to be the application of changing the chemicals within our own bodies in order to become prosperous. This knowledge was handed down and taught from the ancient magi (ancient priests and messengers) citing that whoever wishes to master the principles of alchemy must first master themselves.

In our modern times alchemy is largely associated with the esoteric, spiritual and New Age communities that continue experimenting with ancient knowledge. In previous chapters we looked at how a very select few acquired this sacred knowledge and with it started the New Thought movement. The ethos of the movement adopted prosperity consciousness which allowed individuals to learn ancient perspectives and gaze upon even brighter vistas of spirituality beyond earthly wealth. These alchemical views teach initiates how man was born of two suns. The sun in the sky is the one that nourishes the earth and represented breath. It was thought of as the giver of life that raises all consciousness in relation to ourselves. The other sun is in the middle of our chest cavity known as our solar plexus. It is this internal glow within our body that ancient traditions honored as the key to everything. In ancient times it was thought that the internal sun mirrored the sun in the sky causing a hemispheric relationship between the two solar energies.

Many people pursued the alchemical knowledge of the two suns and spiritual practices by trying to decipher the first instalment from a magical script called the Emerald Tablet. The Emerald Tablet, also known as the Tabula Smaragdina was said to be written by the great God Thoth himself and contained all the power and majesty of creation. In Ancient Egyptian texts Thoth was the ancient Atlantean God who recorded the entire universe on to a tablet. He then passed this wisdom down to the sacred priesthoods in Ancient Egypt. The tablet was green in color and formed from a substance created through transmutation and magic. It was an imperishable object which had the engraving of ancient Atlantean language and other translations on it. These engravings included symbols which responded to the thought waves of the person reading it while releasing a trance-like vibration in the mind. It is said that whoever read the Tablet and was receptive to its power would have their outlook and wisdom increased considerably.

There have been numerous translations and interpretations to accommodate the Tablet's magical teachings. Alchemists highly regard the Tablet as the foundation of understanding all connections to the entire universe. Some people doubted whether the Emerald Tablet actually existed or was just an ancient fable handed down through generations. Deciding whether the Tablet is real or not is irrelevant as there is a valuable lesson via its own allegory. To comprehend and harness the Tablet's true power, one has to realize that the Tablet is actually inside all of us. We have the same molecular mysticism encoded within our thought patterns that replicate the Tablet's codex. In other words, our mind is like a natural sparkling crystal of consciousness but getting this jewel to shine is cryptic just like the stone Tablet itself.

The power that alchemy has in changing people's view of themselves is enlightening. This perspective is so powerful that it guided me to name this point of view as having the Emerald Vision. This vision is the realization that alchemy can assist with changing our view about all our experiences, especially bad ones. Having this kind of vision depends on the current perspective of the individual. When we tap into the deep recess of our thoughts, we can see that true enlightenment is not about being pious or leading an ascetic life; instead it is the act of connecting with who we truly aspire to be with intense scrutiny. In order to elicit those changes within us we must first educate ourselves that the universe is a "one mind" breathing process.

I noted earlier how we humans are taught to divide our reality in our adulthood via separation. There are obviously moments of duality or two sides of a thing in life but alchemy illustrates that these are two sides of one thing. When we start to look at ourselves from this perspective we begin to understand that our ancient masters were teaching us the fundamental key to alchemy. The foundations of this magic lay in accepting that everything is of one whole experience. In alchemy there is a great reference to "the one mind" and "the one thing" meaning that the universe is of one source. The right and left hemisphere of our brain suggests that it is wise to digest opposing aspects but not as two separate things, moreover, as one thing to create balance. Let us put this in the visual context by viewing, for example, the union of night and day as one environmental event. Understand that the day could not possibly exist without the night and when seeing things in this way we are ready to become whole-some, whole-brained and whole-istic (holistic).

Eye Spy!

We are defined by the emphasis we place on our five senses at any particular time which reminds us that we are the product of our environment. Our entire lives depend on becoming rewarded by relativity which is something many of us look forward to in life, although if we desire to be in total celestial submersion with divine intelligence, we should look at returning to the state of a child as mentioned earlier. When we reach the level of questioning, probing and being curious about the world in which we live, just like a child, only then can we can perform miraculous feats. Magicians, sages and shamans have known since the dawn of time how the power of a playful childlike mentality could be utilized to elicit free reign.

None of this is possible if we do not realize that we are constantly evolving in a rapid mirrored existence. This is true when we look at our lives as the infinity symbol that has no beginning and no end. Any part of the symbol can be looked at but its continuum is a constant state of itself. Interestingly, the similarity between the infinity symbol and us is that, like the symbol itself, everything can be moved or reformed because nothing is stationary throughout its path. Therefore, self-transmutation by alchemical definition means that anything you want to change or alter must first be changed within yourself. I feel the need to reiterate that point because our existence is just a reflection of what we are prepared to accept. If we feel that our path lacks any real direction there is a process in alchemy that frees the continuity of any arrested development, and is called dissolution. Dissolution is referred to as the letting go of nuances that do not serve. The image of dissolution in alchemy is the image of two fishes swimming in different directions, which is reminiscent of our lives and our conflicting attitudes. Dissolution in alchemy also has water as an image that depicts the tides of our minds drowning us in our own ego, or washing away parts of us that need dissolving. The alchemical idea is that water is a reflective surface that represents how we can change the flow in our behavior. Water and fire are quite prominent in alchemy and we should understand the importance that these two elements actually possess. They work together as a field of combining their elemental uses which have very similar attributes.

Fire: Fire can burn, yes, but looked at differently, it can burn away unwanted states allowing us to focus and attain clarity. When something burns bright it makes things clearer and shinier, like metal. It is in this burning where we get the phrase "a burning desire" which also means having complete concentration.

Water: Water on the other hand can engulf or submerge by drowning as in the phrase "to drown one's sorrows" but it also can be looked at as washing away unwanted actions.

Losing our way in life is the result of unexpected outcomes

that can lead to uncertainty. We can change the state of our emotions once we learn more about ourselves and the thoughts we entertain that trigger unwanted states. For example, let's say that depression, which is a brain disorder not a mind disorder, can only have real significance to us when we exclusively believe in that diagnosis. I'm not suggesting that depression isn't real, but when we have episodes in the brain that also affect our mind we can enlist alchemy to understand that the elements within us can be changed to release the power within ourselves, so we can feel in control.

So what does alchemy have to do with perspective and vision? I hear you ask. Well, how you do what you do in life is caused by vibrations around you reflecting the images of your thoughts. Using alchemy as the ancients intended is your opportunity to find out how you view yourself. Your vision made perfect, like the word made flesh in biblical scripture, will separate you from your perceived limitations and instead manifest your magnificence. When you realize the power to change your internal viewpoint you will free yourself from your mental constraints. I needn't take you through the systemic formula of alchemy and how the abbreviated symbols are translated, because there is a wealth of information in books and on the Internet that explains their meanings. We are just scratching the surface here and I described this view of alchemy to illustrate how the ancients used this mind power to combat every illusion set before them. Access to this knowledge along with personal transformation revealed, to me at least, that alchemy of the mind is the key to emancipation. How any of us know what we do is just a representation of what we choose to entertain. In a book called *Zen flesh, Zen bones* there is a Zen proverb that states: "You must empty your cup if you are to fill it." This means that you should abandon the things that do not serve you because it is difficult to acquire knowledge when you are already full of knowledge. The same is true with our perception. In order to build spiritual growth we should empty the construct of our "reality" by filling it with a productive point of view. Once you achieve the state of spiritual abundance and recognise your worth and work to be done, your aura will be brighter and all will be revealed to you. It is then the duty of the enlightened recipient to pass on the baton of this knowledge to other seekers, like in a relay race, so they too learn the value of personal transformation.

Positive and Negative Definition

I hope you have noticed throughout this book that I have not used the words positive or negative in describing outcomes. I prefer to use the terms productive and non-productive. In the new consciousness paradigm it is worth elevating ourselves from the constraints of what certain words actually mean. Since we are in the throes of talking about enlightenment, let's look at the reasons these two words – positive and negative – have shaped and misguided our view of the world within our subconscious.

There is a strong universal agreement that the word positive, which can be traced back to the 14th century, originally meant 'settled by agreement' and also of 'absolute certainty'. The denotation confers with the presence of distinguishing thought and unwavering outcomes, like 'being positive', although what does being positive actually mean? Positivity is also synonymous with being desirable, happy and the word 'good'. Words carry emotional resonance and the word positive is no exception as it conjures up feelings of being better than and more luminous than words that oppose it'. Of course words like positive and negative are simple forms of expression when referring to adjectives. However, when talking in terms of valued judgement we should be aware of subjective ambiguity. Associations with the word 'positive' are confidence, practical, optimistic, effective and absolute, to name a few. This being said, we can assume that if the word positive equates to all things being 'good', then the word negative must equate to things that are 'bad'. The word negative also has multiple meanings and usually, erroneously used in the context of whatever is being referred. Research shows that negative is not the opposite of positive. I repeat **NOT** the opposite of positive. The general consensus eludes us to believe that negative is treated as vacuous, dark, sinister and the absence of light.

What negative is has far more descriptive implications than simply meaning not positive. Negative means not affirmative but does not necessarily mean, as in most descriptions, that it is pessimistic, hostile, disparaging, suspicious or expressing malice. It can correlate to being unpleasant but again this depends on its contextual usage. Think about this, in medical terms if you are diagnosed with having certified presence of a dis-ease you would be positive, right? You would hope for a 'negative' result to be deemed healthy. I mentioned earlier that words carry emotional resonance and in this way we acclimate colour and experience to words like positive and negative also. For example the word positive is represented by the colour white and the word negative is associated with the colour black. If this is true (and it is because of its global recognition) then all things that are symbolised with colours and our vocabulary also elicit our emotions.

So you see, negative is not the absence of productivity and to suggest this is crass and perverted because its causes detachment. Enlightened people refrain from seeing positive and negative as separate entities because this thought process can produce adverse effects. There is no definitive proof that white equals good and black equals bad. This is simply a truism and prevalent within our everyday society. This is especially polarized within imagery of the yin/yang symbol and the image of comedy and tragedy etc., just like alchemy. See, now you're getting it! Are we dealing with mere semantics here? No, we are in pursuit of being enlightened. Can I assume that you are reading this book because you seek enlightenment to have greater control over your own perspective? If so, then let us at least exercise accountability for the words that come out of our mouths and the definitions consumed in our minds.

I mentioned earlier that alchemy is one complete experience and how man uses science to create divided thinking. Being scientific results in being thorough, however this thinking also creates irony. For example, Robin Hood we are told, did what? He robbed from the rich and gave to the poor! Well done, you know your nursery crimes! One could say he was positive and was a good man for helping those unfortunate souls who barely survived financially. But hold on a second! Whichever way you look at it, Robin Hood stole riches, which by all accounts would be a bad and negative thing, right? He robbed from the rich and via our perceptive choices we decide that his being a thief is actually a positive thing in this instance. Okay, so let's look at it another way. It was productive in his intention to steal money and give it to the poor but non-productive in leaving those rich folk with a robbed experience – see the difference? Let me use a second example to bring this thought home, especially for those who may disagree with me, which is fine. Anyway, your household cat, domesticated and adored, may be all loving toward you although you would still expect your cat to kill mice and insects. What may be cute little Tiddles to you is a monstrous killing machine in the land of the humble mouse and world of the insect.

In previous chapters I mentioned that prosperity consciousness originally meant that once you acquired knowledge of yourself it would propel you into spiritual awareness. When pursuing social and spiritual power and laws that govern doing things in a certain way, it is wise to return to the teachings of Wallace D. Wattles, who wrote *The Science of Getting Rich*, or read *The Master Key System* by Charles F. Haanel. These books show how prosperity can make you rich monetarily; on the other hand money does not immediately make you prosperous. Once we learn how to turn the base metals of the body into the golden thoughts of our desires, we can wave goodbye to corporeal cravings. These cravings of wanting the instant gratification that money, wealth and riches promise are just the by-product to the person using it as a tool. By investing the time to decipher your own mystery via the principles of alchemy, you will awaken your wealthy character and rich personality regardless. Take a moment and think how the universe mirrors your existence. How can we possibly expect to change our social climate when we furnish our psyche with our current circle? An example of this can be well illustrated when we look at the relationship we have with our friends, loved ones, our jobs and also our environment. Are they not a mirrored extension of who we are? The journey to see the Emerald Vision from this angle starts by learning the keys to unlock the gateway of the body and reap the pastures of the soul.

If your quest is solely for having the abundance of financial freedom, there is a disclaimer. The obvious anecdote of "being careful what you wish for" could only serve to augment your frustration if you misuse the laws of prosperity. Many have tried and failed miserably after ignoring the Seven Hermetic Laws set in the Kyballion by only adhering to one of its laws called the Law of Attraction. When consulting with the universe on such matters of how to gain something, your perspective on life will change dramatically; suffice to say that the path of enlightenment is not for the faint-hearted. Take heed, for celestial rewards are not obvious, nor does the universe contemplate linear time. When you are ready to receive, it will deliver and reflect your endeavors.

"Remember this dear friend, the universe
doesn't mirror what you want,
it mirrors what you already are."

Rico Griffiths-Taitte

20/20 YOU

PART THREE:

All Those In Favor Say "Eye"

HOW TO ACHIEVE THE
PERFECT VISION TO YOUR SUCCESS

CHAPTER 8
Eye Level

In The Blink of An Eye
Look Me in the Eye
Getting Your Eyes on the Prize

PART THREE:
All Those In Favor Say "Eye"

117

Chapter 8:

Eye Level

In my research of how our eyes function I have learned that our vision is a progressive realization of light that shines on to our retina via nerve cells called photoreceptors. Photoreceptors interpret this light and transmit the information to our brain which produces how we see. We can think of our eyes as having a shutter speed like that of a sophisticated camera where every time you blink or move your eyes it takes interpretations, not as one continuous movement but rather snapshots of everything we look at. These snapshots or visual moments are merged to form our field of vision. In fact further research shows that our brain is encased in complete darkness and has no direct contact with light itself. If this is true, then what we see, hear, touch, taste and smell is all constructed via electrical signals which are then entertained in our brain. This suggests that our personal view is subjective and this interpolation is only ever perceived by what the mind develops via our memory and imagination. I promised myself not to get too technical about how our eyes function, although in order to comprehend this visual phenomenon, I'll resign myself to say that our eyes don't see anything at all. As I said, it is our internal five senses that illustrate our external perception. What this means is that the world we see is really just an illusion. We would be mistaken in thinking our world, and indeed the universe, could possibly exist without us first creating it in our mind.

In The Blink of An Eye

When we look at magic or playing card tricks we are told, "The hand is quicker than the eye." How can this be? How can physical movement be quicker than our vision? If close-up magic proves this to be true (and it does) can we ever truly believe what our lying eyes are showing us? It was the American poet, author and philosopher Henry David Thoreau that said, "The question is not what you're looking at but what you see." Assuming that our world is a set of imagined protocols and a sensory play on imagery, let's use an example of someone crossing a busy street to illustrate the illusion of what we see. A man in our example wants to cross a busy street, and after checking both directions may think it's safe to cross. As soon as he starts to walk, a car comes out of nowhere, narrowly missing him. An onlooker nearby might yell, "Look out!" or "Watch out!" What is really being said here is that the man crossing should have been more aware of his surroundings before putting himself in harm's way. He might have seen that it was safe to cross but sometimes our judgment can be clouded. Some people gauge their perception, as in this instance, with a common phrase such as "I swear blind..." meaning we determine what we see with imagined certainty instead of what actually is. This misdirection in what we think we see, especially with our expectations, is what the ancient philosophers taught their students about the principles of visual interpretations, meaning the delusion of reality. They also taught that our belief system and neurological signals form our human perception to believe whatever we choose to believe.

"Believe nothing, no matter where
you read it, or who said it, even
if I have said it, unless it agrees with
your own reason and your
own common sense."

Buddha

While we are talking about what we can see visually, what is not so easy to detect is our own personality, especially when communicating with other people. Very rarely do we display our true character in an authentic way and I say this because the masks we hide behind often protect our personality. Even if the masks are there to protect and control our true feelings, we can certainly disguise our intentions out of fear of being exposed. For example, we are surprised or disappointed when we discover that someone is being deceitful. Moreover, that deceit comes in handy when playing games like poker where you would want to shield your intention and become "poker-faced." When our emotions like rage are triggered it can show a side that we didn't expect to reveal and can be deemed as being out of character. For instance, if you asked a friend who is usually quite placid whether they could display anger at a moment's notice, they may be in discord with you for asking such a probing question. However, what they will ask themselves long after you have parted company is, "Do I really have control over all my emotions?" The answer may be, "No, not entirely."

Look Me in the Eye

Further evidence that the illusion of our eyes are lying to us is illustrated by our modern day TV viewing. When we look at mainstream TV programs of the past there was a wealth of authentic talent that offered moralistic teachings. These lessons provided social tools that we could use throughout our entire lives. British TV shows like *Why Don't You* and *Blue Peter* and American TV shows like *Sesame Street* for example pioneered how children could explore being creative and also improve their moral conduct. Television in days gone by also gave enough light entertainment from multi-talented performers who gave us a welcome break from our own lives. These performers graduated from the ranks of the Vaudeville upbringing, meaning they had theatrical training or were well versed in a variety of performances. This usually meant that they were an all-singing, all-dancing act to be on TV in the first place. However, the difference between that era of television and our modern day entertainment is that we are now inundated with reality TV shows. Of course you have your own opinion about this genre and make of it what you will, but for a great many people reality television invites the viewer into a world they wouldn't otherwise see. We as a human species seem to strive for acceptance with our immediate surroundings, and watching reality TV indicates a kind of social empathy for the characters on screen hence why these shows are so popular. The question we should ask ourselves about reality TV is that if watching everyone else's life makes "good television viewing" then what does it say about our own lives? Is watching "real TV" a glimpse of our potential? If so, are our own lives not considered to be real? If the premise of these shows is to build a relationship with the on-screen characters, there is usually a contradiction between what we see on the screen and our own real world experiences. What we must not lose is our connectedness to who we really are. It seems that our real lives are constantly determined by either intention or attention. The operative word is tension and the pressures of the human experience are alleviated while watching "real world television." The key word here is escapism and watching reality TV evidently shows an insatiable thirst for the armchair voyeur.

Our past gurus and luminaries didn't have television to

entertain themselves in ancient times; their form of entertainment included connecting with nature to propagate their spiritual thought process. If we are to follow in their transcendental footsteps it is best advised to emulate a similar connection to nature for our own spiritual awakening. Watching other people's lives on TV should never affect our search for our own purpose in life. This purpose should start with us learning to eclipse the ego so that we don't become judgmental. I mention this here because so many of us have taken on the role of a social observer. We assume that we have the right to judge others and feel superior to those who air their problems on TV for our entertainment. Although the prosperous ones among us have realized that once the ego is relinquished of its duty to feel exalted over others, we can truly benefit from the Latin phrase *"nosce te ipsum"* which means "know thyself."

We often think that the road to prosperity should be a smooth path of releasing our emotional bondage to gain spirituality. This is far from plain sailing as the path to enlightenment, known as the state of personal insight, can take a second to apply but a lifetime to master. Let me add a determinist point of view. Determinism is a philosophical idea or movement citing that everything is for a reason and has an inevitable consequence. Therefore, the view of the devout determinist is that we should explore our own potential because we are the very idea that predicates our actions. As I said before, to know thyself is the first thought, the first intention or idea of having a natural proclivity to be liberated by our desires. In short, learn every facet of your abilities and it will grant you control and liberation. Even the philosopher Spinoza wrote that "freedom is the recognition of necessity." Yes, we need to feel freedom to be in control but do we also need pain, suffering and loss to experience feeling alive? For example, someone may use the phrase "pinch me" to affirm whether they are in a dream state or awake, which seems to suggest that pain equals purpose. According to the practice of Bodhisattva, meaning one who follows the ways of the Buddha and its teachings, we should embrace that living is not completely without suffering. It is us humans that create the divine promise in ourselves and choose our own state of reality through our point of view.

Previously I only touched upon the subject of how the Ancient Egyptians had advanced knowledge about the power of the mind through their internal and external viewpoints. The Predynastic Egyptians (before Egypt was so named) had an invested interest in proving that having knowledge of ourselves was the basis of how an individual could reflect the universe in his or her existence. In other words, if you wanted to be harmonious with the universe you first must understand that:

YOU ARE THE UNIVERSE

If you do not comply with this outlook you will never benefit from your own agreement. Let's first break down what your mental agreement looks like etymologically. The word agree means to be to one's liking or to one's own pleasing, also to give consent, originating from *ad+gratum*. Ad: toward something; gratum: grace, favor or virtue. So by your own virtue you should align yourself with who you are naturally as you have agreed in your own mind. The decision to be authentically true to yourself in every situation can create a more harmonious image that reflects how you feel inside. Let me ask you a question. Have you ever seen an old photograph of yourself and thought: I didn't know I looked like that? Whether we are pleased or surprised by the photo, we tend to have a different perspective of how we see ourselves versus how we look to other people. There is an industry specifically assigned to people who require visual dexterity with their personal or professional image. It is called image consultancy and the consultants are experts in creating an image of how a person would like to appear to others.

We should look deeper at the reasons why people accept their own illusions set before them, especially in pursuit of their goals. These reasons often start when we ask ourselves questions about our personal gain of any pursuit. Questions that plague us like, "What will happen if I achieve my dreams?" is just as worrying as "What will happen if I do not?" Being faced with these types of questions can result in a stalemate if we are afraid of the outcome and choose to do nothing. This non-productivity can seriously hinder and arrest our desires, whereas the answer lies in us removing the blinkers from our mind's eye to reveal the whole spectrum of intent. The answer might be that we need to center ourselves. The answer is we need to get focused.

Getting Your Eyes on the Prize

I would like to draw your attention to a word that denotes the essence of pure clarity, reason and supreme thought, and that word is behavior. Every sage, rishi and guru all formed synergy with their desired outcome via behavior. From Shaman to Lama, Buddha to Brahma, it was always the intention to become one with the divine principle of "becoming." To comprehend this becoming means to assimilate and acclimate with who you are by being natural, being reverent, but just be. This is true of all the laws of the universe.

In ancient times a prosperous person had knowledge of the world and also the star systems with a productive outlook about all things both natural and supernatural. To achieve this "becoming" starts with learning ancient laws which were given as a set of instructions to govern your natural well-being. Knowing these laws, according to Pharaonic scripture, meant that your actions on Earth prepared you for the other realm known as death. Death also meant paving the way to ultimate paradise, which was known as returning home to your original source of light. The laws of living harmoniously with nature, knowledge of polar opposites (masculine and feminine energy) and the preparation of spiritual connection were revered. In essence, before there was a law of any modern day metropolis, the ancients had lore, folklore to be exact. This meant that a person who could see the divine principle in everything was indeed a prosperous person. In ancient times, this universal lore was easily accessible and more sophisticated which heightened your connection to nature; therefore, from the enlightened masters of Atlantis to the pagans and initiated priesthoods of Ancient Egypt, it was necessary to guard this knowledge until one was ready. This knowledge was unique and called Sophia by the Ancient Greeks. The word Sophia means wisdom, which at the time was also associated with the word occult later endorsed by the Wiccan religion. The word occult simply means hidden knowledge and our ancient teachers knew that this knowledge in the wrong hands could be a very dangerous thing. That's why specific training was necessary in order to acquire wisdom.

Throughout history there have been countless examples of how to achieve wealth along with what it truly meant to be financially liberated. During the 1900s the American author Napoleon Hill reminded us, "Whatever the mind can conceive and believe the mind can achieve." He gave us the tools that wealthy people used and still use to this day. However, knowledge of how to become rich or wealthy doesn't appeal to everyone and yet two questions deserve answering if you expect to profit from using this knowledge of the affluent:

1. *Can everyone achieve success, be rich and lead fulfilling lives without financial worry?*

2. *Is having the abundance of money our ultimate freedom?*

The answers may be a unanimous "No!" However, our modern day self-help gurus and motivational speakers tell us that we can be anything we want to be. The empowerment industry is churning out more life coaches than the self-help circus can actually handle. It's moving at a rapid rate exponentially with authors, websites and seminars aplenty revealing the process that our ancient masters held only for the esoteric few. Now stadiums are packed with seekers of the truth hoping to hear the person who stands before them say something that's both life-changing and anecdotal. Since the release of books like *The Gospel of Wealth* written in 1889 by Andrew Carnegie, and *The Master Key System* written in 1916 by Charles F. Haanel, these manuscripts actually served as blueprints to prosper from by using Hermetic wisdom.

As powerful as the message was back in the 1900s, it was later popularized and credited for its commercial guise as Rhonda Byrnes called it *The Secret*. The book *The Secret* borrowed a slice from the Hermetic texts and used just one of its laws, namely the Law of Attraction, to illustrate how to get what we want via positive thinking. *The Secret* as a book and subsequently the movie made modern day gurus of its presenters. It turned the whole prosperity machine into the reawakening for prosperous living. There were, however, considerable chunks of information not discussed in the book or the movie. The application of just thinking of what we want and then receiving it is decidedly utopian. However romantic an idea it may seem, just thinking about the prospect of wealth doesn't guarantee that this actually works, nor does it authenticate that everyone can or should apply it in the suggested manner to be successful. I have no personal issue with the message in *The Secret* but it seems that a great number of people felt the representation of the movie lacked authenticity and appealed solely to consumer naiveté. Ancient teachings, where these "secret" laws originated, are to be respected and it would benefit us greatly if we considered every lore of the cosmos, as described in the Seven Laws in the Hermetica. Truth is there was never a secret. It was common knowledge in Ancient Egypt and Predynastic times to live with moralistic values and productivity. There was nothing extraneous or unnatural about the science of lore. In fact the science was quite exacting and its path was taught to those initiates once they turned a certain age. Besides that, it was cultural living that set the richness of Ancient Egypt apart from anywhere else in the world at that time. Students of these schools of thought were shown that having perspective delivered the entire universe for spiritual balance and not just a Law of Attraction that led to material gain.

This process of thinking positive or productive isn't wrong; however, it does require a great deal of personal conviction and self-worth through evidence. Interestingly, it was Martin Luther King that said, "We hold these truths to be self-evident," taken from his 1962 speech, and in fact it is self-evidence that pervades your perception when achieving your dreams. What we have at our disposal is inside us which liberates higher levels of consciousness. Our ancient masters of this thought process wanted us to understand the power that we already possess. Once we have unwavering faith in ourselves and we dare to dream, only then can we possibly have the right to be enlightened.

We just traveled down the historical path of prosperity. Now it's your turn to see the spiritual map of a road less traveled. In the next chapter we will look at how **YOU** can create your own path to awareness, but first you need the key to achieve consciousness mastery.

CHAPTER 9

Innervisions

Trusting Your Point of View
See Me!
Visionary Questionnaire
What is the Third Eye?
Developing the Third Eye
Third Eye Activation: The Process
Enlightenment

PART THREE:
All Those In Favor Say "Eye"

Chapter 9:

Innervisions

We are all unique individuals who share many commonalities in our wants, needs and desires. However, what is usually undetected is that we also have within us hidden talents and knowledge that need exploring and, because of this uniqueness, we owe it to ourselves to express being different. Once we entertain that prosperity is an overflowing river that we can bathe ourselves in, we can expect to be rewarded for those differences by creating our own significance and set our wheels of enlightenment in motion.

Trusting Your Point of View

Our world is a grand illusion constructed through our own perception and recently it has become increasingly evident that the world we know, or think we know, presents challenges that can apprehend our inner brilliance. As I've said before, changing our perception gives us an opportunity to look at things differently. However, there are times when society unfairly criticizes just how significant we can actually become, especially in our pursuit of being unique. If we use the fame industry as an example, there are countless people who are multi-talented and brilliant, yet some people never have the opportunity of expressing their talents to the rest of the world. Actors, performers, artists, or those wanting to excel in academics for that matter, have all expected to see the fruits of their visions manifest and become a reality. Suffice to say that not everyone achieves their dreams, and unfortunately when reality bites this can leave us feeling disappointed. To further this point, when we do not get the opportunity to live out our desires or earn a living from our chosen profession, this can be hard to accept as some people painstakingly invest their time into honing their craft. Talented people could say that not being given the opportunity to excel is somewhat unfair, and they would be right in thinking so. We often question why situations are unfair but unfairness is prevalent throughout life. If we concentrate on whether life is fair or not, we risk losing our main objective which is to find our real purpose. Anyone who expects to be recognized for his or her ability will see a familiar contradiction that is presented to us in modern society. That contradiction cannot be ignored when we see how other less deserving, less talented people seemingly blossom. How can this be? Surely talented people should be able to profit from their passion, shouldn't they?

People come up with all kinds of reasons why they do not achieve their dreams but the number one reason seems to be a "lack" of something. People use the excuse of lack constantly, blaming lack of resources, lack of time, lack of knowledge etc. There is a big difference that separates prosperous people from persistent ones. The answer lies in the opportunity to believe in every angle of your abilities, as prosperous people do. The difference is in your choice whether to persist in using lack as an excuse or prosper from it. Prosperous people know how to handle bad news, unfair decisions and conflicting issues. Followers of prosperous thinking have tunnel vision no matter what level of distraction or hurdle they face. What's wrong with being persistent? I hear you ask. Absolutely nothing, except that having a persistent mindset reduces your options to see opportunity everywhere. When you adopt the mindset of "when you have lemons, make lemonade" you cast out accepting "lack of" and replace it with "learn from." This will place you immediately in the seat of knowing that everything is for a greater purpose and a greater reward awaits you. This is possibly where the phrase "Where there's a will, there's a way" came from because this is how prosperous people think. They are strident in their need to make a difference in their lives by having a wider scope and realize beyond reasonable doubt that they are not victims of any circumstance but instead a student of having greater self-awareness.

The marvelous thing about having this inner vision is that once you adopt the power of self-awareness, not only will you be in line with your highest potential, you will acquire a more grateful satisfying gift of prosperity. If we look at the movie or music industry, those who receive awards and accolades for their craft usually attribute their success to many things. The fundamental truth lies in them having unwavering faith and devotion in themselves or a higher force, which is why they are exalted. Let's take the example from that amazing musician Prince when he was interviewed about his childhood days. He expressed that when he was young and dreamed of his aspirations as an adult, he said, "Come what may, I was going to get a job in the music industry." His intention to entertain all possibilities of doing at least something music-related opened himself to conquer all. We know how that process turned out for him and the rest, as they say, is history.

When you know what you want and consequently what you don't want in terms of achieving, it means that you will be part of the elite, known as an exalted person. The universe is your guarantor to your promise and adopting this mindset will expose you to *brilliance,* which is why you shine or stand out as being the best at what you do. It's no surprise then that the most famous or celebrated among us are called "stars." In order to emulate people who have this kind of outlook you must lead and motivate yourself in knowing every facet of your being. You can start achieving this by asking yourself the following questions:

- ▲ *If prosperity had a flavor, what would it taste like?*

- ▲ *How would I feel if I were prosperous?*

- ▲ *What does prosperity sound or smell like?*

- ▲ *How would I behave knowing that I am a prosperous person?*

- ▲ *How do others react to me now that I'm prosperous?*

Remember, there is no right or wrong answer. Understanding and entertaining the answers to these kinds of questions is the cornerstone to being brilliant. Others will be inspired by your ability to control your persona and of course you could become successful, if this is what you seek. Remember you are the recipient of that which you desire most. However, we should not have a short-sighted view on becoming publicly recognized or famous. Expecting to be rewarded for behaviors rendered is not out of being grateful, deserving or focused, it just shows pomposity and arrogance, which are egotistical. The pursuit of stardom can be harmful if you do not balance the responsibility that comes with it. We should consider a broader view of being famous as there are many people within our own families and in our communities that deserve to be credited as stars in our daily lives. These local superstars guide and shape our environment and it is these unsung heroes and heroines that need recognition also.

See Me!

The principle of knowing who you really are starts with you developing a relationship with your celestial self and learning to let go of things that bind you. Personal release or letting go is ultimately the real freedom of fearful outcomes. It is this letting go which you experienced while in your mother's womb when you were a mere fetus suspended in the water of wonderment, without a care in the world, just allowing yourself to be.

> "When you come into the life just as yourself, surrendered and open, you're not a program not on some mission, you just are."

> **Mooji**

For my own recognition of this liberating feeling of letting go, I interviewed 10 people who do extreme sports otherwise known as adrenalin junkies. I only wanted to ask two questions for this research. My first question was, "What do you feel when doing these activities?" and my second question was, "How do you feel when you are not doing these activities?" The 10 responses I received were of no surprise at all. They all confirmed that while they were in full active mode they felt a mixture of fear and happiness and, at the same time, a feeling of being alive. For example, when I questioned some rock climbers, I could see their eyes light up as they recreated the moment while describing what they felt. Their responses were a mixture of "It's frightening but I feel free" and "I forget everything else around me." I interpreted their description of this feeling to hang-gliding, skydiving or swimming, which is comparable to the same sensation recreated inside our mother's womb. That feeling of being suspended and surrounded by nothingness is the act of pure patience, love and abundant feeling of "being alive." The suspended self is what we are trying to achieve here and once you start to acknowledge this weightlessness, the process of knowing how good you really are at being you and being true to yourself will greatly be enhanced. All doubt will begin to diminish and this learning to accept the whole self, complete with idiosyncrasies, will help you to, as the Americans say, "get over yourself" and find gratitude for all that you are. Your life will inevitably become more prosperous and you will realize the huge difference between being concerned with self and being self-ish. Let's look for a moment what the etymology for the "self" actually means. The word self refers to a said person, which comes from the old English "sylf" or "self" meaning "one's own person."

The wonderful mind that is Eckhart Tolle says this about the self:

"Your sense of self comes not from thought but the stillness of thought. The presence which comes out of consciousness of who you are. Once you know who you are at this moment, your life situation is of relative importance. It is of relative importance whether you are poor or wealthy, if the body is healthy, if you have satisfying relationships, whether you have a nice place to live or an unpleasant place to live, it all has importance but it is not of absolute importance. Know who you are beyond the forms."

The integral part of knowing who you are is by looking at your circle of influence and your surroundings. Take a good look at your friends and the company you entertain. Look at your job and how it makes you feel. Look at your current relationship and notice what it's made of you. Also look at your eating habits and you will see yourself mirrored; suffice to say you behave like the food you consume. Ever heard the phrase "You are what you eat"? This is the universe serving to mirror who you really are.

There is an old African proverb that translates into different languages but its interpretation is the same. The phrase is an example that stems from the Ubuntu philosophy to the Asante that states:

"I am because we are, and because we are, therefore I am."

This proverb means the representation of who you are is reflected in the company you keep. Your environment can easily influence you if you are not connected to your inner guidance. This path of internal wisdom is also known as your intuition, internal "sat nav" or following your mind. The leaders of the New Thought movement and prosperity consciousness of the early 1900s knew that abundance is pervasive. I mean, even the ancient master teachers knew that the divine principle of wealth was omnipotent and omnipresent, meaning everywhere. Let us not make the mistake of thinking that rich people are prosperous and poor people are not. A rich person with a seemingly fortuitous upbringing can have a poor mindset; also a person that does not have much money can be extremely rich, not monetarily but spiritually. The one common denominator will always be our perspective and each one of us can easily switch places in an instant. This proves that our mental attitude is the only thing that defines how we behave and knowledge is the only thing which separates all of us. This stems from an aptitude that you knew before you entered this earthly paradigm. The elixir of that knowledge was light coded and evolved into liquid crystals known as blood. That's right! This knowledge flows through your veins, together with the inhalation and circulation of your breath, and forms the lock and key to your molecular make-up.

> "Everyone thinks of changing the world, but no one thinks of changing himself."

Leo Tolstoy

Recently a friend of mine approached me looking really depleted like the light had gone out of his being as he told me that he felt depressed. I said, "Great, teach me how to do that." He looked at me confused as you can imagine. I was intrigued how he knew this diagnosis even without going to the doctor. I paused for a moment then I asked him, "When you were a baby how did you get out of being depressed?" Still looking confused, he answered, "I wasn't depressed as a baby." I then said, "How do you know you weren't depressed?" I waited as I could see him recalling those times, then he smiled and replied, "I know I wasn't depressed because anything that I wanted, like food, I got it." As he mentioned food I decided to stay with the subject and went on to ask him what actions he took to acquire food as a baby. He had this slight smirk on his face that led to a realization of his own genius as he answered, "I cried when I was hungry and I got fed." I observed his physiology and noticed his instant acknowledgment that even when he wanted to be fed as a baby, he decided to be proactive and he was duly rewarded. But didn't we all do that at some point? We all knew how to ask and receive and even though crying really isn't the preferred way to ask for anything, it got the attention and the result we wanted. I wasn't trying to trivialize my friend's statement that he was depressed nor did I want to say that it was imagined. He obviously felt this emotion and it was very real to him but I wanted to find out how he acknowledged what he said he was feeling was in fact depression. As I asked him questions about his state as a baby it seemed that a light came on in his mind as he remembered that in order to get what he wanted he took action. The point here is this is something that he had always known. Somewhere along life's highway, he had fallen victim to ignoring this internal knowledge he was born with which then became dormant.

We should all reacquaint ourselves with having this knowledge by synthesizing with what we desire. All too often we depend on something to happen to us before we take action, like waiting for enough money to appear or miraculously expecting there to be more hours in the day than the day before, for example. In actuality our inner wisdom comes naturally equipped with having spiritual dominance and confidence in ourselves to be abundant. Let's look at the definition of the word confidence. The word confidence comes from the Latin vernacular of *con* meaning with and *fidence* meaning faith. So literally it means "with faith" in our deeds. I have summarized this process with this statement:

"When you have faith in your decisions you make the right decisions."

Rico Griffiths-Taitte

You have every resource available to you in achieving what you desire and this is absolutely the master key in knowing thyself. That's what your ancestors knew and that's what they want you to know also. You may be asking yourself, "Well that sounds good, but how do I go about achieving knowledge of myself? Where do I start?" The good news is that it started when you decided to ask these kinds of questions and took the first step in reading words like these:

"When you take one step toward the Guru, he takes a million steps toward you."

Sikh saying

Visionary Questionnaire

The purpose of the following exercise is that once you start asking yourself the questions below you will build an image that has been dormant in your subconscious for some time. Answering these questions openly and honestly means that you can start entertaining your future state of what's needed to forge ahead with equanimity.

Exercise

Take a piece of paper and create a table like the example below. Write down your answers to these questions leaving out no detail. List all the things you discover and really take a moment to analyze your answers. This can greatly help you address issues and leverage those behaviors that no longer serve you.

Question	Answer
1.	

Answer the following:

▲ *What do I see when I look in the mirror?*

▲ *When do I know when something is working out the way I planned?*

▲ *How do I view my relationships with friends and loved ones?*

▲ *Do I see a less than average, an average or a better than average outcome when I attempt something?*

▲ *How do I feel when others seem to be more fortunate than me?*

▲ *What do I feel when others react productively to every situation?*

▲ *What benefits are there to being productive?*

▲ *What would it mean to me if I lived my life with purpose?*

▲ *What would others say if I looked like I lived my life with purpose?*

▲ *How can I make myself appear more assertive to others?*

▲ *What do I need to be completely right about something?*

▲ *What would my favorite character, actor or person I admire do in my situation?*

Now ask your friends and relatives the questions below:

▲ *When you look at me, what do you see?*

▲ *How do you think I see myself?*

If you have answered the above questions honestly you will begin to get a better, clearer picture of how you appear to yourself and others. Next, visualize changing areas of your traits that you feel need attention or enhancing. You may be surprised to find there are areas that you like about yourself. What we are creating is the blueprint of uniqueness and by focusing on the things that you can do rather than the things that dampen your spirit will reveal new adjectives that describe your essence. This process is the foundation of the real you coming through. Once you challenge yourself and find your inner revelations it will lead you to your own path of enlightenment. Once you have tweaked the person in your answers, look at the new avatar of yourself. After a week or two, read your answers over again and you will be surprised with what you have created. Your new vision of who you would like to be will give you new tools to start impacting the rest of your life. People whom I have asked to answer these questions have said that looking at their traits written down empowered them in order to find their true calling.

One of the main keys to enlightenment is learning how to use your imagination. The benefit of using the right hemisphere of our brain, which is the creative side, means it is conscious enough to embrace things that may be out of the ordinary or not logical. The left side of the brain is the logical side that processes information. However, what we are looking for is the perfect model of who you have invented so you can open the doors of your perception, even if it means playing let's pretend. When you become your own image consultant and build your new persona it might feel strange paying so much attention to yourself, however, treat this not as entertaining the ego but use it in preparation to create your uniqueness. Even the most amazing celebrities have the ability to reinvent themselves with the help of stylists, don't they? Once you have completed the previous exercise, place the paper somewhere high so you can admire it. Read the list of your new image and make it a morning ritual to remind yourself of what you represent before you step out into the world. Use it as a successful personal playbook for every eventuality you are aiming for. Embrace becoming an individual and if people do not treat you the way you expect, then teach them how to treat you from now on. Take notice of how people react to you because you have taken notice of yourself. Top business people, entrepreneurs, elite actors and actresses, even top Olympic athletes, have one common trait with their personality and that is they envisage how they want people to see them in order to succeed.

"When people see your personality
come out, they feel so good, like
they actually know who you are."

Usain Bolt

Once you look at your internal illumination and challenge yourself, you will cultivate a new projection of your personality. That illumination begins with your third eye.

What is the Third Eye?

The mind's eye, more commonly known as the third eye, allows us to experience visions and other mystical phenomena that lead to a door of endless possibilities. Learning to open this door might just be the greatest test of our mental agility we will ever discover on this earth. How we go about accessing this power is not for the faint-hearted and if it is to be activated it first needs to be identified.

The third eye, also called the pineal gland, is a small endocrine gland that produces melatonin, which is a hormone that affects the functions of sleep. The third eye, which is located between the two hemispheres of the brain, is the size of a pea and its shape is reminiscent of a pine-cone. Once this gland is opened it can transport us to an advanced perception beyond our ordinary vision. New Age spirituality cites that meditation techniques are the best way to open the full power of the third eye although being intuitive and creative can also access its potential. The invocation of opening this gland can differ from person to person, as the experience is uniquely personal. Some people experience hearing a popping sound and immense pressure in their brain before realizing that the gland is active, others have reported their third eye opening completely by accident. Of course we know there are no such things as accidents and what this tells us about the power of this awakening is that once it is fully exposed, one has to be ready to adopt a new way of seeing.

Our perception exists between our imagination and our level of consciousness, and by opening the third eye you can access your psychic ability, clarity and spiritual connection to the universe. What I would like you to comprehend is that this gland does not see an outward projection as we do with our physical eyes; it is instructed to see inner consciousness, because everything is inner consciousness. Many ancient civilizations understood the spiritual workings of the third eye by entertaining its enlightening power. Through third eye activation they realized it was possible to alter consciousness, create healing and shape reality via synthesizing with its energy. In Hinduism, the third eye is referred to as the Ajna or brow chakra. They also regard the third eye as the gate that leads to inner realms and spaces of higher consciousness. In New Age spirituality, the third eye often symbolizes a state of enlightenment or the evocation of mental images with personal spiritual significance. Third eye activation is also associated with having the ability to observe chakras and auras, precognition, and out-of-body experiences. People who claim to have the capacity to utilize their third eye are sometimes known as shamans, light-workers and enlightened beings who can use their universal vibrations to manipulate its energy.

Developing the Third Eye

An opened third eye produces a third dimensional world of wisdom and illumination, which is relayed by its results. How you go about translating those results depends on your ability to interpret the images that you receive. Proper relaxation techniques are advised before integrating with its practices, and when we have moments of true intuition, the pineal is said to vibrate gently, opening your inner eye and illuminating your soul. Any questions of doubt about your existence will be answered once you expand this spiritual intelligence. Some people have commented on seeing past and future events, others have reported experiencing unconditional love and being very sensitive to other people's emotions. There are even those who have discovered a hidden talent that immediately opens a gateway of how to express themselves. The beauty of this is that your connection to seeing this way will start to have major significance to you and you alone. In order to initiate our multidimensional consciousness and expand our gateway into the other realms, there is no hard and fast rule about what you can expect to see once it is opened.

In my quest for initiating my own third eye experience, I heard sounds and saw colors that revealed concepts and images which were not predetermined thought patterns. Even now while I'm being creative, like when I'm sitting at my drawing board or while playing my guitar, I experience universal instructions coming from the guidance of my third eye being activated. I don't really know how to explain this, but it feels like my third eye is continually open. Even during sleep I find myself waking up and having an automatic need to grab a pencil and start drawing or writing something down. I see things much clearer and, for reasons I don't care to rationalize, simply documenting what I am being exposed to guides me to appreciate the mind's inner brilliance. For the artists, designers and authors among you who can relate to this, you will know that while doing something creative, your breathing pattern is at its most peaceful state. In fact any action that requires concentration will connect you to this tranquil experience. When you are most relaxed, it is during this state where you can feel guided into other dimensions. While I am doing anything creative I feel that there is no sense of time, as if time didn't exist at all, and I guess this is where the phrase "time flies when you're having fun" comes from. It should comfort you to know that the introduction to higher consciousness appears courtesy of knowing how to let go of earthly expectation; especially with your third eye activated, anything that your subconscious wants to direct you to is where you should follow.

Be careful of indulging the ego while trying to awaken this powerful gland as it can bring false promises of grandeur and limited self-control that weakens the spirit. We should take responsibility for things that block our third eye, in particular our intake of certain foods and also information that serves to taint the mind. Also distractive thoughts and even toxic people can abrade our endeavors to become enlightened. Anything which isn't conducive to your journey can interrupt your motive for reaching your higher purpose with the universe. Whatever capabilities lie dormant within us will suddenly be enhanced when opening the third eye. Like Neo in *The Matrix* when he realized true enlightenment, you will also become illuminated and change your outlook of your existence. Be receptive of this liberating doorway by allowing this endless flow to fill you full of wonder of this mysterious force. This is why it is important to monitor your thoughts and the foods that you consume. When you consume new ways of behavior and redirect your focus, only then can you open all the wheels of your being.

The third eye is very powerful in its awareness of our natural volition. In fact I don't refer to the pineal gland as the third eye but rather the first eye, as it processes information germane to what you want it to see. After its assessment of whatever you imagine, the information is relayed back to the other senses, shaping what we call reality. Once the cosmic unity of the pituitary and pineal glands are opened it is so powerful that it can literally drive some people insane if not fully understood, accepted or developed correctly. Some people are afraid of opening this porthole, therefore they suppress its functionality because it can be used to alter patterns we are accustomed to.

When we facilitate third eye activation we can enhance our intuition which can also make us better decision-makers. From the moment we wake up to the time we go to bed we are constantly making decisions. Scientists have identified areas of the brain that involve decision-making and it is generally accepted that all of our decisions are based on self-interests. When the third eye is activated, synthesizing with your decisions is without doubt the most conducive arena to learn about who you really are. How we arrive at making our decisions includes many factors, even decisions made by other people affect our own decision-making. Our choices are subjective and when attempting to open the third eye for clarity or enlightenment we can embrace inner knowing so that any uncertainty of "what if" is replaced by "what now." True mastery of having imagined outcomes in decision-making is a very magical skill that requires insight.

> "Living is a constant process of deciding what to do."
>
> **Jose Ortega**

Third Eye Activation: The Process

Let's look at the process of third eye activation. You can start by sitting upright in a chair so that you feel grounded or in a cross-legged position on the floor with a cushion for support. Ensure that you are completely comfortable before attempting this as you are going to be traveling without constraint. Next, close your eyes and focus your attention at the point between your eyebrows. Monitor your breathing pattern, which should be evenly regulated each time you take a breath. Ignore any distractions arising from your environment and within your body, remembering to make a point of just sitting in the present moment. This method is best practiced when it is really quiet. While feeling totally grounded, next focus more intently on your presence. Be aware of your posture and thoughts that materialize. You may begin to see lights or colors emanating from this process and soon recognize images that identify themselves as the very essence of consciousness. Practicing to open the third eye does not need to be an intensive process as some people suggest. For starters, not everyone has the same experience but know that just by attempting this process you are calling to your higher self and you are being beckoned to open the spectrum of light inside you.

Interestingly, the porthole to the higher self is best practiced when we go to sleep because the mind is allowed to entertain a relaxed mode of consciousness without physical restriction. Sleep takes you through many situations and dream states whether you remember them or not. You can also open your third eye by daydreaming which is conducive to seeing higher states of consciousness. Another way to achieve third eye activation is through concentration and focusing during meditation. Some people do this through yoga meditations that align your attention with your focus. The essential form of this mediation holds its principles in the astral planes. When you have tried this a few times you may want to record your findings. Take notes of what happens before, during and after your attempts which may prove valuable in how you connect to your higher self. The most important thing to know about ascension is that this will be the culmination of everything you have experienced up to this point in your life. While doing meditative practices, incantations or mantras, you may find that your concentration wanders. This is totally part of the experience – however, don't stop, even if you fall asleep during these attempts. It does not mean that you are doing something wrong or that it's not working, but instead it may be that your subconscious has found another path. When you are not in the mood or frame of mind to initiate this process, it is advised to practice more relaxation techniques remembering that the pineal gland is activated by frequencies of calming tones to the ears. That being said, listening to meditative music is ideal and even more effective through personal headphones.

Enlightenment

Being enlightened, or opening all our chakras for that matter, it's not what most people think it is. I have stated before that we are all individual and I still adhere to that because we are most certainly connected by our auric fields in the great web of our existence. One typical way that is practiced worldwide and favored for third eye activation is by being in a dark room and just relaxing. A great number of textbooks cite that sitting or lying down in the dark reveals the benefits of seeking enlightenment. When practicing this way, be aware of any sensations or experiences of flashing images around you. It is important to let your inner vision see what your physical eyes do not. Accessing and trusting your higher intelligence and knowledge is your intuitive self-evolving. It is now up to you to learn the purpose of its unlimited power and learning how to access it develops your higher state of consciousness. Most of the material available to purchase on opening the third eye always points to an arrival of an end result. As I have said before, the expectancy to see something materialize creates the delusion of you not being enlightened. You must realize that you are from the source of light frequency that beckons you "NOW." Even while reading spiritual literature you must know that you are being called to meet your true inner purpose. All you must adjust is your perception of what it takes to return home to that source. This is a new time period and we are incredibly more awakened than ever before. The forces that tried to apprehend our path to ascension in the past are diluting which means we now have quicker access to our prosperity.

Certain mantras can be chanted which can help to open up this power of enlightenment. Deep breathing exercises like that of Pranayama bring the breath or chi (energy) up to the third eye area, which is also beneficial. Soothing music possesses tones and frequencies that help release tensions in the body and rejuvenate the mind. Scents like frankincense, myrrh, sage, lavender and essential oils in aromatherapy are ideal for stimulating the third eye also. Last but not least, your diet can initiate spiritual awakenings in this area. A diet high in meat, dairy, complex and refined starches, sugar, salt, etc. will greatly impair this pathway to opening enlightenment, as well as cigarettes, alcohol and drugs (legal and illegal). Even being deceitful or fraudulent will close the porthole to enlightenment and become wasted energy. Learn to approach these practices by first learning to let go of any thoughts and ideas that hinder you. Thoughts like fear, doubt, jealousy and envy should be relinquished and abandoned as these do not serve you in your attempt to raise your consciousness.

To awaken anything that you want on a higher plane should be developed and assisted by a happy disposition in your life. Understand what annoys you and then learn to remove yourself from those energies that arrest your development. On this journey of self-discovery you might find that you will feel resistance from those around you because of your chosen path. Proceed with caution as people with non-productive energies and entities can suppress you. This may sound strange to the student at first but your hang-ups and ego-based circles create resistance so it is wise to seek protection while trying to rise from the ashes of your former self. Whatever you get as a reward from these practices is priceless to you and you should know that access to this brilliance will become brighter the more you apply it. You will also find that your psychic awareness increases as you eventually awaken your inner guru. You will start to notice how your life becomes incredibly distant from your former self and you will automatically rebuke behaviors in other people that are not conducive to you anymore. You will, however, attract more openness and calmness, which may surprise you as you become extremely powerful.

Focal Point

LOOK OUT: Opening the third eye is about seeing, both literally and intuitively. This is the chakra of visions, dreams and imagination. If this chakra is closed we are easily beguiled and confused. Without this clarity or activation we can also experience having no direction and find that we live without guidance. The worst that can happen is that we live without purpose. Departure from your old habits means that you have tuned yourself to a frequency that cannot possibly restrict you.

PERSPECTIVE: This is a very liberating process indeed and the rewards of third eye activation are bountiful. It is important to be mindful of what you experience; for example, your vision may lead you to see miraculous things that seem impossible. If you are doubtful about what you entertain, the answer might not immediately make sense to you because of your perception of uncertainty. When you begin your journey with this power, it will reveal to you only what you take into your subconscious. During this time your personal issues will also rear their heads and show you your true being. Your mind will always highlight with what you convince yourself to be real. Before we reach the state of clarity some people are unprepared with what they see during third eye activation as their personal truths might emerge and frighten them. This leads to shocking and unsuspected results and because of this we need guidance in the face of fear while seeking arenas of enlightenment.

Luke Skywalker: *"I won't fail you, I'm not afraid."*
Yoda: *"Good, you will be, you will be."*

Seeing The Light

More Than Meets the Eye
The Power of Concentration
Concentration Practice
Enhancing your Focus
The Benefits of Gratitude
Seeking Gratitude
The Key to Gratitude Mastery

PART THREE:
All Those In Favor Say "Eye"

Chapter 10:

Seeing The Light

When you continuously visualize an image in your mind, your body radiates and generates precise images. These images subconsciously synthesize with said thoughts on both the physical and non-physical levels. The frequency of these levels attempts to unite you toward your desires while moving everything else out of your way to manifest what you are entertaining. This is the power of visualization.

More Than Meets the Eye

The latest studies in neurosciences reveal that thoughts interact with the same mental instructions as actions. Mental imagery provides a preview of what you can expect from an actual desired outcome. Athletes who envisage winning or being at the top of their profession use planning, preparation and visualization to achieve greatness. For example, Muhammad Ali constantly reminded the world that he was the best at his craft by stating "I am the greatest." This served to ignite his passion for his profession which he entertained in his thinking process. I hope you realize that training the brain to visualize enhances motivation, increases your confidence and produces noticeable self-improvement.

We can see through the power of the Internet that many mentors and holistic gurus alike talk about the benefits of visuallzatlon. This ethos is borrowed from the Hermetic laws in a "see it and achieve it" context. The fact that scholars of universal law promote this use of imagination is very persuasive as they remind us to "imagine the thing we desire most then watch it magically appear." I advocate visualization techniques and even hypnotizing yourself into believing in your abilities. However, the average person who just thinks about their dreams and expects to be duly rewarded will soon realize that this only produces temporary results. As I have previously stated throughout this book, your point of view is a significant factor between you and achieving your desires. This all depends on how much creativity you administer. Prosperous people receive the benefits of using their imagination to continually manifest their desires. They know that if you are not physically being interactive with your imagination it will only serve to destroy what you worked so hard to build up. For example, how many of us know someone who just talks about their goals but never acts upon them? It seems that these individuals need motivation to get things started, but more importantly than that, they need concentration.

The Power of Concentration

"The only way to keep from going backward is to keep going forward. Eternal vigilance is the price of success. There are three steps, and each one is absolutely essential. You must first have the knowledge of your power; second, the courage to dare; third, the faith to do."

Charles F. Haanel

Concentrate: Comes from the Latin word *con* meaning with and *centrum* meaning center, placed together, it leads to condensed mental focus. There are those who suggest that we are not born with the ability to concentrate and that it is a skill which needs to be acquired and developed. Some proclaim that we are taught many subjects in school but how to concentrate isn't one of them. This is a short-sighted opinion because when we do our research we see a large number of children from different cultures that are trained to concentrate on daily duties. Duties like doing housework, otherwise known as chores, are preparation for a child to be a well-rounded and responsible adult. The notion of having this kind of duty at a young age has spiritual overtones with the universe. This also has everything to do with the cosmic flow of productivity and connection to divine principles. It is possible that the western hemisphere observed and adopted the saying "Cleanliness is next to godliness" from watching and learning from these cultural practices.

You could say that a child should be allowed to be a child and you would be correct. The fact still remains that when a child is given the responsibility of chores, they can acclimate very quickly and very naturally on how to be a responsible adult later on in life without being forced. I would just like to state that in no way or fashion would I advocate pushy parenting, although I absolutely encourage exemplified parental guidance. The imagination of a child should be cherished and applauded as it is as powerful as any Law of Attraction known to man. A child's mind can entertain many a cosmic utterance and still remain childlike and brilliant (I should know, I used to be one!). I can tell you that even when a child's mind seems to wander, they are still aware of their surroundings; they are just entertaining a different set of instructions from a different realm. It seems that as we grow into adulthood we seem to forget about our imaginary friends that we communicated with in our childhood in exchange for us becoming sensible and logically astute.

With what we now know about the word concentration, think about something that you really enjoy doing most. No naughty jokes please! While you're doing something you enjoy, are you not automatically concentrating on it? The act of concentration not only means the ability to direct our attention to something, it also means having tunnel vision about a particular act. Prosperous people surround themselves with what they expect, which is how they orchestrate abundance flowing to them. They do not discount all other possibilities; they just know how to be centered. To concentrate means you are prioritizing something. That's where many of us lose sight of our ambitions. We need not exclude all other sensations, thoughts or ideas; we just need to center ourselves to put things in order of importance where it becomes a priority. The word priority means to be on top.

Although the mind should be allowed to wander to entertain all possibilities, guided concentration gives us the ability to have mind power and control over our thoughts. What we're really talking about here is control, and in order to profit from this process requires much training. Being raised with the values of concentration is advantageous although there are those who lack the ability to guide their attention and focus the mind exclusively on one subject. Concentration is a natural skill and not unfamiliar to us, we just forgot how to do it. Concentration is a sacred action and once you apply it in your physical, mental and spiritual arena your route to prosperity will be increased immensely. It was the Master Indian Siddhar (Saint) Patanjali that said:

"Peace can be reached through meditation on the knowledge which dreams give. Peace can also be reached through concentration upon that which is dearest to the heart."

Concentration Practice

Meditation is a brilliant way to center yourself and a perfect aid in controlling your thoughts in order to embrace your whole being. Here is an ancient technique which has inspired many meditative practices globally and acquired many names over the years but originally was simply known as The Way.

Take a deep breath and try this:

Take a moment to sit alone in a comfortable position so that you are not tempted to adjust yourself. Before doing so, you may want to light a candle, burn your favorite incense and put on some gentle music, preferably sounds of nature. Posture is important, so sit in a comfortable chair placing your hands palms down on your thighs. This is the best starting place to initiate stillness. Using a candle is helpful in this instance to learn how to concentrate on an object.

Place the candle where you can see it relatively close, like on a table in front of you, and focus your awareness on just your breath. Regulate your breathing allowing the mind to focus on the light and energy that emanates from the candle. Half close your eyes and soften your gaze, meaning don't forcibly strain your eyes to see. Keep your concentration on the flicker of the flame as you get lost in the moment. Don't worry if your mind begins to wander, that's part of the process. You can do this with your eyes closed if you prefer, especially if you are visually impaired. All I am stating here is that with your eyes closed you can imagine a flickering flame to give the same results. Gazing on a single point of light expands your ability to zone into other realms. Without moving your gaze, observe your peripheral vision. You may see a blurred image and even the candle might appear to double in picture, this means you are in full meditative state.

You are an elemental being, and during this time ask of your chosen divinity to unify all the elements of nature within you. As your imagination dances with the flame, allow yourself to just merge with it and perhaps you could see your own image as the candle itself. Lose yourself in its unfolding of whatever images come to mind. Do not rationalize, or legitimize anything, just notice the presence of being focused. You have now laid the foundation of concentration. At this point start thinking about your desires. That's all there is to it. I like to do this in the early hours of the morning when all around me is quiet and the world seems peaceful. Once this synthesis is achieved you can begin using the above technique of concentration with everything. After a while you will find that you no longer need the candle at all as you automatically begin to align yourself naturally. This technique can be applied to anything which you want connection with. You can apply it to having your chosen lifestyle or job you always wanted, even the kind of relationship you desire. You can perform this anywhere even on your daily journey. For example, as you go to and from work you can call upon the ability to slipstream Into concentrated thought by getting that faraway look in your eyes.

Caution: Obviously this must not be attempted while driving or doing things that require concentration!! Get it?! Sorry, I couldn't resist using that pun.

Our minds beg to be challenged every second of our lives yet we are constantly showered with things that distract us. The art of meditation is based entirely on doing nothing more than concentrating. While in a meditative state, it is suggested that we take notice of the thoughts that enter our mind. Some say think of nothing but this is not what we're trying to achieve. Thinking of nothing will only end up with you thinking about how not to think of nothing! Phew! You want to get creative with your thoughts and start picturing yourself where you want to be, which is to center yourself.

Have you ever been on a train and while looking out of the window you just drift off as if you are oblivious to everything else around you? That is the same result you want to achieve while concentrating. Mindful awareness inspires us to concentrate upon all other areas of our lives, and once you have clarity of what you want and what you don't want, your concentrated thought will result in the following:

▲ *Your goals, objectives and your memory will improve.*

▲ *Your perspective on your life will be clearer.*

▲ *When making decisions you will quickly have clear, defined answers and desired outcomes.*

▲ *You will not become easily distracted as your mental acuity will be sharper.*

▲ *Your thoughts will be more creative and you will quickly dismiss unwanted imagery.*

▲ *Your other senses will also be more alert. Being open to this process will make you pay more attention.*

▲ *You will begin to see possibilities that you were otherwise blind to before.*

Enhancing your Focus

There is no etymological origin for the word "focus" other than to directly center on something. What is interesting is that researchers have traced the word focus back to when it was used to describe looking at fire. In ancient times, pagans and mystics would stare into fires to manifest a spiritual revelation, which is still known today as scrying. Shamans and mystic priesthoods would stare into various reflective surfaces, e.g. water, to perceive past or future events, which is similar to our modern day crystal ball gazing. Scrying, which means to see images in a reflective surface, is believed to reveal unseen things to the initiate. Perhaps the origins of the word focus originally meant concentrating on a particular center point of activity or energy.

The underlying theme of concentrating on what you want is one thing, but once you have focus how do you maintain it? We can view focus like this:

F = Find

The etymological explanation of the word "find" is from an old English word meaning to meet with, discover; obtain by search or study. When you search and find whatever you deem a goal or objective, your determination will be rewarded with an authentic sense of achievement. To find yourself first is the beginning of that which you are looking for. It was the philosopher Rumi that said, "Whatever you seek is seeking you."

O = Opportunities

After you have found yourself you should ask the question: How do I associate with other prosperous people? It may surprise you to know that all prosperous and successful people always want to be around others who are like-minded so that new and profitable opportunities flourish in their chosen arena.

C = Create

You have achieved the ability to concentrate. Now here comes the fun part. You have to be creative in different situations especially in scenarios that you want to work for you. This is the stage where even the most famous and influential of people reinvent themselves or create a mystique to build upon their dream.

U = Unique

As they say in business: What is your unique selling point? Okay, so you have drive, ambition and you set your sights high. What also has to be high is your profile. For what reasons should anyone take interest in you? What do you have to offer? Even being in a small concentrated crowd you have to find your niche which will make you discoverable in your uniqueness.

S = Synergy

Synergy is a natural process combined with focus. An idea

by itself is just an idea, but an idea plus action and focus is an unstoppable fusion.

Using the above process we can see that with concentration and focus we enter a world that prosperous people have employed since the dawn of time. Just to round this up so you can see how it centers on your goals, it can be said like this:

"Prosperous people are focused through the intention of desire."

Rico Griffiths-Taitte

Focal Point

LOOK OUT: If you see yourself as having conflicting situations, they will consume you until you concentrate on productive outcomes.

PERSPECTIVE: Learning to diminish outcomes that do not serve you is a unique skill. We can start by not surrounding ourselves with the things which hinder us. When you are armed with the tools to divert your attention and busy your mind, undesirable results will appear to take less prominence over your emotions. This is the time to get creative and see what else can be done for your imagination to manifest.

> "You can't depend on your eyes
> when your imagination is out of focus."

Mark Twain

Next we have to look at gratitude because nothing works better in tandem with focus than being grateful for everything.

The Benefits of Gratitude

> "Happiness cannot be traveled to, owned, earned, worn or consumed. Happiness is the spiritual experience of living every minute with love, grace and gratitude"

Denis Waitley

The word gratitude is Latin in origin, coming from *gratus* meaning pleasing or thankful. Like the word grace, the origin of this word is from the Latin *gratia* meaning favor, esteem, pleasing quality, of good will and gratitude. In old French it means divine, mercy, favor, thanks, elegance, virtue, thankful and pleasing. There has been a lot of scientific research on the subject of happiness and the prerequisite of it seems to be gratitude. The key ingredients for allowing us to lead fulfilling lives and being prosperous are giving thanks and being respectful about everything. I cite these as having three effective benefits:

The three benefits of effective gratitude are:

1. Appreciation

Gratitude is consciousness of all things acknowledged. It can help us to practice forgiveness and know for example that you couldn't possibly be hurt when you appreciate pure love. Hurting yourself with destructive substances only serves to poison the mind and trigger your emotions like doubt and hate. However, when you learn to appreciate who you are as a natural being, you embody the definition of being eternally loved. Yes, appreciation transcends even painful experiences and heals the heart.

2. Impression

When we express gratitude it opens the whole chakra system by activating wheels of productive neurons in the body and impresses upon any spiritual practice. Our mind is pre-set on a regulated pattern of repetition, physical acquisition and motor skills, and once we take a moment to feel grateful for everything we attempt, it affects what we want with authenticity.

3. Productive Emotions

Scientists have studied that having gratitude can change the way our brains are wired. These productive emotions awaken a kind of knowing in us that at our most fundamental level we are happy. The word happy or to be in "hap" means to be in with a chance or to have options. Some people might state categorically that they are not happy, but if they are shown what they do have instead of what they do not, it can make them appreciate so much more in life, opening more possibilities for prosperity.

The advantage point

Make it a daily routine to sit and prostrate (kneel down in reverence) with your own mantra and simply start your day by saying thank you. Doing this is very liberating to know that you are in the presence of allowing yourself to be humbled. I personally give thanks every morning by simply waking up (that's a good start to any day) and then sitting on the edge of my bed and think about the gift of my breath. You too could start early in the morning by thinking about your achievements and being thankful before starting your morning duties. This will ripple productive things to look out for throughout the rest of the day. While you are in your grateful state, take a moment to think about what you are capable of achieving from morning to night. If we look at the word capable, it comes from the Latin verb *carpere* which means to capture or seize. It is possible that this is where the expression *carpe diem* (seize the day) comes from. Be grateful for many things both productive and non-productive, because both of these words denote action and movement.

Seeking Gratitude

According to the ancient principles, when seeking gratitude you will come to know that:

▲ *You have always been rich and had access to the well of abundance.*

▲ *You feel the universal connectedness reminding you that you are not alone.*

▲ *You are thankful for challenges because without them how would you feel victorious when you overcome them?*

▲ *Your productivity will increase.*

▲ *You possess the ability to create a climate of other like-minded people.*

▲ *You will appreciate guidance from your ancestors as you become aware of being supported spiritually.*

"Let us be grateful to people who make us happy; they are the charming gardeners who make our souls blossom."

Marcel Proust

Finding joy in every situation demonstrates your level of gratitude. No matter how insignificant the act is, being grateful reminds us of the productive things in our lives. If you cast your mind back to when you were a child, hopefully you can recall a time when you received that unexpected Christmas or birthday present. To the loving parent or guardian it didn't matter how they acquired the present, they would have moved Heaven and Earth to accomplish it and the only thing they cared about was that you received it with gratitude. Have you ever heard people complain about their jobs? Well, in this financial climate we should be grateful to at least have a job to complain about. As research shows, having gratitude impacts everything around us greatly. The practice of gratitude is one of life's most valuable lessons. It shifts your focus from what you lack in life to what you already possess to be grateful for, like the gift of unconditional love.

Behavioral and psychological therapists can attribute that there is a surprising improvement in the quality of life when we practice gratitude. Giving thanks makes people happier and more resilient.

It strengthens relationships and improves health exponentially, even reducing stress. May I suggest that the practice of being grateful be aided by writing things down to be grateful for and it might even be worth keeping a gratitude journal. There is a wealth of templates and ideas of how to start a gratitude journal all over the Internet and also many books have been written on the subject. People have been known to use this exercise to appreciate things when in times of doubt, fear or being distracted off their path. Some people wait until the end of the day or just before they go to bed to write down what they are grateful for. Even if you only list five things that you learned and are grateful for in just one day, this can serve to make your future outcomes more productive. The purpose of this is to see your accomplishments visually and record your own personal commitment to greatness.

I went through a deep sense of self-loathing when I lost the use of my left eye. Many years later I learned to forgive myself and I now accept that had it not been for that experience, I probably would not be able to see as I do now. I now call my new sight "seeing with grateful goggles." It has also augmented my ability to appreciate being able-bodied to do more creative, instinctive things without fear of failing or doubt.

I expect there to be some cynics among you who would question: How can you be grateful when something bad or unfortunate happens to you? If we cast our minds back to the section on loss in Chapter 6, we can question why things affect us, but when we start appreciating life by applying gratitude it can assist with achieving a state of clarity. In the face of adversity we should be asking: How can I learn from this experience? To help us cope with feeling conflicted during these times we should be aware that gratitude is heightened when we change our outlook. The lessons that emerge during these times make us learn to acquire better insight. The phrase "everything is for a reason" may have been right out of the stables of gratitude. Remember, in the gardens of difficulty there are the seeds of conscious benefit. There is a solution to adversity but first you need The Key.

The Key to Gratitude Mastery

Once you begin to align yourself with being grateful, your inner knowing of things wished for will embrace you immediately. We have previously discussed that there is nothing external of self, and once you comprehend this you can declare yourself the recipient of grace. What gratitude is not is the act of just thanking the rewards for things desired. Getting what you want with no gratitude can lead to ego myopia which means being out of focus with what you already have. Let's highlight our understanding and appreciation by saying that gratitude is:

▲ *Watching the rain fall from your window and seeing it cleanse the earth.*

▲ *Watching your children while they sleep knowing they are safe in your care.*

▲ *Stroking your beloved pet.*

▲ *A hug from a loved one.*

▲ *Waking up to see the dawn.*

▲ *Getting good espresso coffee.*

▲ *Soaking in the bath tub.*

When you notice the little things like having running water, or even something as simple as laughter, you constantly look for gratitude in everything. Gratitude is also when you have been turned down for a job that you really wanted but you didn't get, just so you can find an even better, more prosperous position and career.

I was recently in Paris, France and around 8:00 am I left the hotel and sat down at a nearby café. I was welcomed by a palpable smell of freshly baked bread. Oh my goodness! The smell of fresh bread was piquant and its aroma put me in a state of gratitude. I ordered a croissant and as I took the first bite into the slightly warm crunch of the pastry, the feather-light dusting of sugar was accompanied by the soft velvet of the almond paste that melted in my mouth. The taste took me back to my childhood as I remembered being awakened by the heartfelt tones of my grandmother's singing from the kitchen downstairs as the smell of breakfast filled the air. Do you see how gratitude can even transcend time? You can't be miserable while being grateful.

A word of warning when dealing with gratitude! Do not wait for a productive outcome in order to feel a grateful state. If you are faced with disappointment, this is the universe's way to appoint you a new view of learning. I would like to point out that contrary to a lot of books on the subject of the Law of Attraction, where people believe that the universe always works on your behalf, there is a mild disclaimer at the bottom of your celestial contract. The fine print states that even though the universe has your best interest at heart, it also has a strange sense of humor and a very warped sense of irony. For instance, a person that you love might end a relationship with you for many reasons but you might not be aware of the purpose of its demise. However, when the hurt is gone you may feel immense gratitude because you finally appreciate the reasons why it was necessary for it to end. Of course I'm being whimsical but let me illustrate this point further. The universe may let you fall in love with the wrong person just so it can teach you that you may love "too much" and lose yourself when in love. By removing you from this experience of loving too much, the message could reveal that you are too co-dependent and needy. The purpose for this revelation might be to assist in developing balance with your emotions, enabling you to find a truer, deeper, meaningful connection with your intended soul mate as well as yourself. To see gratitude in this way and use it with focus puts you in the seat of ultimate consciousness. Once you understand this point of view you will be in line with becoming a master of divine grace which is the key to your enlightenment.

"Be in a state of gratitude for everything that shows up in your life. Be thankful for the storms as well as the smooth sailing. What is the lesson or gift in what you are experiencing right now? Find your joy not in what's missing in your life but in how you can serve."

Wayne Dyer

The Vista of Enlightenment

Sightseeing
Seeing Things Differently
All Those in Favor Say "Eye"

PART THREE:
All Those In Favor Say "Eye"

Chapter 11:

The Vista of Enlightenment

Neo: *"I can't go back, can I?"*
Morpheus: *"No. But if you could, would you really want to?"*

The Matrix

If you have stayed with me this long through our journey of self-discovery and visual acuity then I believe that you are ready to receive the most potent secret from ancient teachings known to humankind. In the pursuit of higher knowledge it may seem difficult at first to elevate ourselves to the level of higher learning, especially if we don't know what that level is. However, one thing I can assure you is that the splendors of being awakened will deliver your personal freedom sealed with an abundant knowing of your purpose on this Earth. This is the absolute truth that I mentioned in the introduction to this book. The reason people even start their intrepid journey to enlightenment is that they sense there is something else out there. That "something else" concurs with their curiosity about their own existence. Evidence of that curiosity is replicated in

177

many other explorers who also traveled down the same road of unsettled questioning. The inherent beauty of self-discovery teaches us that the more you learn about yourself, the more you disengage from the confines and illusions placed upon your mind. Choosing to what extent you interact with that illusion will be entirely your own decision. Moreover, if you decide to dip your toe into the waters of ancient thought, it will submerge you in your unfettered desire to be enlightened.

Let's start this spiritual anointing with the connotation and denotation of the word enlightenment. Even within the spelling of the word lies the molecular vignette of the master key. In the word enlightenment the en- represents the word *inner* and *lighten* is the state itself that shines your soul's essence. Simply knowing this shows us that ancient knowledge is laden with coordinates that are hidden in plain sight and is the key to the human mythos of enlightenment.

In preparation for writing this book I researched why so many arguments were diverse on what it means to be enlightened and live a prosperous fulfilling existence. I discovered a host of books that describe how to acquire wealth and how to adopt a behavior that couldn't possibly fail you. I subscribed to most of their teachings, although it was my quest to find the origins of this thought process even before there was something called success or wealth. I started searching from as far back as the ancient texts all the way to the modern day motivational speaker. What I found was a simplistic knowing of ourselves and the human experience that is overlooked in most present day literature. If you see yourself as a bit of an Indiana Jones and you go digging for the golden treasure of knowledge, you will eventually stumble upon one simple rule that had been staring you in the face all along. That rule is what the ancient prophets reserved for selected students, which was never the intention to confuse anybody; you just had to possess a great deal of open mindedness for the revelation to higher consciousness. It is the one thing that the ancients wanted us to realize with their cryptic pictograms, symbols and monoliths and the message was this:

"You are already the thing you are trying to become."

Rico Griffiths-Taitte

I hear you saying to yourself: Surely it can't be that simple, can it? Oh yes but it is; however, you must learn patience, young Skywalker. I have been honest in my attempt to reveal the journey to self-discovery set by ancient teachings, but I hope you can see for yourself that even within its simplicity it first requires profound training on your part. Next we will see how to pick from the tree of truth and knowledge so you can profit from these lessons and master your own vision.

Sightseeing

If you truly seek enlightenment you will need to engage in experiential practices to see the benefits. It is fundamentally important to be interactive with the idea of being spiritually liberated instead of just reading books on the subject. If you just read about the state of enlightenment and do little else, you will only fill your mind with ideas and expectations that support a self-confessed illusion, bypassing the experience of enlightenment entirely. There are wonderful books that can help you with small epiphanies but do not expect them to take you to your destination of perceived freedom, even within this book. It is best practice to elicit the assistance from productive literature along with your own judgment to support your ascension. The importance of being proactive and creatively enlightened will result in having fun with what you discover about yourself. You should expect the universe to afford you having a wry sense of humor, even sarcasm, as you become more playful and see the lighter side of your true calling.

Throughout this book we have been traveling down the yellow brick road of curiosity, now let's pull back the curtains to reveal the real wizard of us. The question you may be asking yourself during your journey could be: How will I know when the principles outlined in this book have made me enlightened according to ancient philosophies? You will know when you are on the path to enlightenment when:

▲ *You stop comparing yourself to others.*

▲ *You know that you are no more important than anyone else.*

▲ *You know that no one else is more important than you.*

▲ *You treat yourself with the utmost respect.*

▲ *You treat everyone else with respect.*

▲ *You distance yourself from those who refuse to respect you.*

▲ *You accept that everyone is different and not equal.*

▲ *You will find that people who connect to a higher consciousness do not try so hard to be seen or heard*

▲ *You will listen more than you speak.*

▲ *You will seek not to make an impression on anyone, as process is better than popularity.*

These 10 attributes will place you as the master of your inner sanctuary. Once you practice and attain these principles, and make up your own, the world will seem like a different place and your internal point of view will change dramatically.

Seeing Things Differently

When something motivates change in us we know that something mentally must also change. What is happening in our psyche is that our perception is becoming enhanced as we see things differently. For example, when we hear words of encouragement it uplifts our self-worth and we experience empowering thoughts which alter our usual patterns.

When we apply the views from the previous chapters and really open our eyes as well as our minds, we invite reverence into our line of sight. Seekers of enlightenment are both reverent and empathetic, and learning to accept every facet of these applications also makes you more appreciative and, in turn, more prosperous. When we adopt compassion and reverence for each other it shows us how to be more respectful and become more holistic. The word reverence comes from the Latin *reverendus* or *reverentia* meaning to be worthy of respect. Reverence also by definition is someone who is worthy of being respected. That could possibly be the reason why a clergyman is called Reverend. Reverence leads to adjusting the way you behave which shifts any limitations about the way you think.

We should look at being more creative rather than being stuck in a logistic pattern. For example, I used to work in the city and every day I waited at the train station for the 7:00 am train going to London Victoria. I, like many people, would wait on the platform in the same place I always did to get on the train and sit in my preferred seat. I started to notice a repeated pattern with everyone who would perform this same ritual every day at the same time. Then one day I noticed a young lady who stood near me would always arrive at 6:55 am with the utmost determination to get to her particular place on the platform. She would literally rush to get to "her spot" as if her life depended on it, then push and shove her way to get on the train and sit in "her seat" and do her make-up. This routine started me thinking about how habitual we have all become. One day I purposefully left my home earlier than usual, arrived at the station at 6:50 am, stood in "her spot" and waited for this lady to arrive. Sure enough, like clockwork, she arrived at 6:55 am. When she saw me standing there, the look on her face appeared aggressive – in fact, if looks could kill I'd be writing this from beyond the grave. She looked confused as she was forced to stand behind another passenger. When she got on the train and sat down, I saw that this lady who was still looking confused managed to sit in her chosen seat and do her make-up as usual. The point here is that we are all guilty of having repeated motifs in our lives because it places our subconscious need to be in a system. That system is also known as a state of inertia. I know, I know: if it ain't broke then why fix it?! But my reason for changing my position with this woman at the train station was not to disturb her pattern but to illustrate that society dictates how we live our lives by expecting everything to run on time, like a train schedule. If you doubt that idea, the next time you are at your spot on the platform of the train station (see, you do it too), notice the response from people around you if the train is delayed or the journey is disrupted. Disruption can occur when traveling because of course anything can happen to alter our journey, but the same is also true along our journey to enlightenment.

Doing things differently may be the only way of understanding how to break the mold of any repetitive cycle. Our enlightened masters always changed ideas and altered points of view via experimentation. They knew how to manipulate required behaviors by being flexible while being true to themselves as the Divine intended. I would just like to point out at this time that I have used the word divine on a number of occasions, 26 times to be exact. The word divine is just another way of saying your denomination and should be applied accordingly. Actually, divinity is another way of saying universal intelligence, which is our blueprint for being prosperous.

People repeatedly ask me, "If our ancient masters were so knowledgeable about the universe then what happened to them, and why did they fall?" Well, my answer is always the same as I remind them to "open their eyes." I say this because we can marvel at our ancient masters' prowess just by looking around our own cities. There are countless ancient symbols sprinkled throughout our sprawling metropolis. All of this imagery in our contemporary world pays homage to higher consciousness and the very symbols themselves depict mastery of ancient innovation. We could spend a lifetime wondering what happened to those ancient masters and where they ended up, but the rise and fall of those great ancient minds and cultures only happened because they wanted it that way. What they left us as tools to advance our own journey was but a blade of grass compared to their fields of spiritual awareness. Although it is hard to accept this fact, the only way to mend our current ignorance is via all of us traveling with divine intention whilst seeking knowledge. This universal frequency of spiritual intelligence has our compass firmly set to what is known in certain circles as the collective consciousness.

I remember starting this chapter in the week leading up to December 21, 2012. That date was significant in the ancient Mayan calendar which predicted the world would end caused by a great flood. A few close friends wanted to know my thoughts on the subject as they asked, "What do you think about the prophecy of a great flood covering the earth and killing millions?" I said, "Yes it is true. What

I can tell you from my own personal research in metaphysics is that there most certainly will be a great flood, a deluge in fact of oceanic proportions which is going to be cataclysmic in its wake. The water will cover the entire earth." They were stunned by my response but I continued by saying, "Oh yes, I hope you all can swim in this flood, but it will not be water as we know it. There will be a new tidal wave of consciousness that will cover the earth, cleansing vibrations that do not serve us anymore. This new wave of enlightenment will be the letting go of a great many things. People, places and events will fall away from the ones who seek true enlightenment. Even relationships will falter as the new consciousness paradigm attracts you to adopt a better frequency of purging and letting go of circumstances that intoxicate the mind, body and spirit."

Of course we now know that the world didn't end when the Mayans predicted. I remembered how those around me questioned whether they should do something productive with their lives with the little time they had left. However, on the very next day there was a universal sigh of relief when this prophecy of a great flood didn't happen, or did it? No, the world didn't end but the Mayans didn't mean it would physically end either. You see, now more than ever is the time for the truth to emerge and rise from the sea of deceit, especially within ourselves. Modern day metaphysicians, pagans and leaders of the New Thought movement knew that a great deluge was never meant to enlist fear, just welcome a new wave of consciousness.

If the prospect of suffering the Mayan's oceanic catastrophe frightened you at that time, you should have had faith in the cosmic agreement that in order to awaken and cleanse any old paradigm, a spiritual flood is imminent. Seeking enlightenment means that what we feed our intellect through our senses will reveal the behaviors of people around us also. What will emerge is that you will filter out those people whose agendas are different from your own. As your senses become heightened, things that you entertained before which led you astray from reaching your goals will have no more significance to you. You will begin to synthesize with your own being and it will be the start of something magnificent; however, some people can experience suffering during this time, as the road to enlightenment often elicits your own personal truths that many people just cannot seem to accept. Rest assured that revealing these truths will be rewarding, as overcoming our own personal constraints must be dissolved to purge obstacles that apprehend us. When we expand our consciousness we can become more enlightened, but that level of conscious liberation does not stop at washing away the sins of our thoughts, it is the way we live our entire lives. There are some students who learn these principles as young as five years of age and others who learn it at 65. Age is not important because enlightened people do not rest on the merits of when it will happen; they just know that it will. Once you declare yourself aligned with the principles of knowing you, the whole you, and nothing but the you, nothing can sway you from your path. Nothing and no one can possibly tempt you to return to your old habits that do not serve your path to enlightenment.

"Neo, sooner or later you're going to realize just as I did that there's a difference between knowing the path and walking the path."

Morpheus - The Matrix

All Those In Favor Say "Eye"

According to etymological books, the definition of the word real translates as actually existing, true or relating to a certain thing.

One notion suggests that the word real originated in Latin as meaning genuine. Real is quite obviously a subjective experience and we need not enlist the help of anything external of ourselves to determine our reality. What we choose to entertain is a personal point of reference until we decide otherwise. However, let me give you an example of a calcified mind that believes it is owed the splendors of enlightenment because of what someone thinks is real.

During the summer of 2012 I attended a conference about spirituality where the speakers talked about out-of-body experiences and such. After the speakers had finished, we all had the opportunity to mingle and talk among ourselves. A lady introduced herself to me and then went on to refer to matters of the universe. She had adorned herself with amulets and was wearing a flowing tie-dye purple and orange dress that reached the floor but was just long enough to show the sandals she was wearing. While she was talking, she felt the need to tell me repeatedly that she was "a deep person." The need to present herself that way was visually obvious and it was also apparent that she liked talking, so I let her continue. She told me that she was spiritually connected and I thought to myself: Okay, when someone has to tell you that they are spiritual and deep, they are probably anything but. She went on to say that her understanding of universal law and its rewards baffled her as she had tried everything to become a famous writer but wasn't getting the results from the Law of Attraction. She went on about the movie *The Secret*, which was the topic of choice at the time, and she also talked about what was "real magic." I slapped my forehead and said "good grief" to myself! I remember thinking that understanding the Law of Attraction is one thing but applying it and expecting it to just magically deliver because you want it to is complete ignorance. I had to stop this lady mid-flow, so I said, "Er... miss, there is no such thing as magic, there is only that which has not yet been revealed." She looked at me very confused. I went on to say, "If a trick or illusion was ever revealed to you then no longer would it be shrouded in mystery."

You too may have looked at me with raised eyebrows as she did, but I expanded upon my statement by using what I call "the artist in front of a blank canvas theory." Let me explain. What does the artist sitting before a blank canvas initially see before making a single stroke? Do they see a blank canvas or a piece of art that is not manifested in the physical realm? Just because an image isn't drawn yet doesn't mean it isn't there. Let's look at the etymology of the word draw. The word draw comes from the Old English word *dragan* meaning to drag out. To make an impression on paper or canvas it has to be dragged by an implement to leave its mark. The word draw also means uncertainty as in a game with no definitive winner, which then becomes a draw. In essence, an artist with the implement of a pencil or brush has the hallmark of a magician playing with many possibilities, making something that was invisible now visible; the unseen, seen and the unreal somehow come to life. The lady finally agreed that in order to comply with the Law of Attraction we must first illustrate a specific picture in our mind so that our desires can be drawn into existence. The key to understanding my "artist in front of a blank canvas theory" should begin to show you that we ourselves need to be the artists, composers, designers and architects to orchestrate greatness from within. Nevertheless, as I said earlier, this requires much training for it to manifest.

As I said at the beginning of this chapter, you will see the splendors of being awakened and see your truth when you become centered. For example, if you stand in a bookstore and connect with your higher self you may find that some books call out to be picked up and read. This tells us that we are connected to higher frequencies via our curiosity and by being open to receive these frequencies helps us to realise that our ancestors are guiding us to have specific knowledge at our disposal. You will come to learn that their assistance will show you the path you are looking for by way of putting certain people, situations, and in this case, even books in front of you to show you the way. Your ancestors have always anticipated you asking for their support, as they do with all initiated souls. They simply want you to raise your hand as they request, "All those in favor say Eye."

How to See Sight Beyond Sight

All Eyes on Me

PART THREE:
All Those In Favor Say "Eye"

Chapter 12:

How to See Sight
Beyond Sight

I want to end this book with the beginning, the beginning of all thought and creation, the initial source of our being even before we experience the external self. Inside the word self are the letters E and L which are the coordinates to our higher being. This EL is significant in remembering where we came from and aiming to get back to in order to communicate with that higher intelligence. In some ancient cultures the EL was the name for the highest divine being, the alpha and omega or simply known as the "all and all." In the ancient Hebrew language the EL was a generic word for God as in the name The Elohim which was used to describe a singular supreme God. The ancient Canaanites also referred to the EL as God being the father of mankind and all creatures. I illustrate this because we can see our own embedded mastery inside the power of the EL or s-el-f, even before we were born. We evolved from the EL principle and somewhere along life's highway we lost our way in search for the self. Let us remind ourselves that in the dark embryonic stage of our mother's womb there was an entire fertile existence all of its own. In fact it wasn't dark at all, it was pure brilliance and light-coded with spiritual awareness. From luminescent tadpoles that swam on mass frantically trying to make it through from our "father time" (man) into "mother nature" (woman) where only one cell is needed to make it, we can see that we emerged from magnificence. When you see yourself from this point of view that one stellar cell completed its mission where thousands did not and consequently died, you will appreciate that simply being here on Earth and being alive is in itself quite miraculous.

When we think about the beginning of our creation in this way, it is evident that as we grow into adulthood our porthole of light gets increasingly narrow and we lose the coordinates to our universal "stargate" where we originated. This is what the influential Russian spiritual teacher G. I. Gurdjieff was teaching with his fundamental message about self-remembering. Gurdjieff taught his principle of how man was constantly losing himself in search of his own purpose. There's nothing wrong with being lost but our journey in life is largely dependent on being found through that which defines us. That journey of being found should have started with the nature and nurturing from our parents who really knew us well before we knew ourselves.

Parental guidance means being accountable for what we expose to our children, especially in early development. According to epigenetics, which is the study of modifications and functionality of our genes, it is suggested that our thoughts, likes, dislikes, fears and successes are passed down intravenously to our children via our mindset and biology. Even though children may grow up and form their own experiences, there is a natural inheritance for them to follow suit. If our thoughts and even our habits are passed down to our offspring, this means we should periodically remind them of how potentially brilliant they can be also because they came from brilliance. Their ancestral lineage paved the way for them to exist, suffice to say that we are all the personification of our ancestors complete with their behaviors until we awaken our own patterns and identity.

"Awakening is possible only for those who seek it and want it, for those who are ready to struggle with themselves and work on themselves for a very long time and very persistently in order to attain it."

G.I. Gurdjieff

Searching for an identity can take a lifetime; however, in essence you can't completely know where you're going until you know where you came from. As children we didn't need to search for this identity because we were too busy being childlike. What I mean by this is that as adults we spend an inordinate amount of time trying to be adult about things, just so we can appear logical and responsible without contradiction. However, all too often we forget how to just be ourselves (remember we talked about masks in Chapter 7). This need to legitimize everything in adulthood shows how quickly we dismiss the proverb on the walls of the ancient temple of Luxor in Egypt where it stated: "Man know thyself and you shall know the gods." That proverb was engraved upon the outer temple where initiates were allowed to come and learn about their natural internal powers. The second most inner part of the temple had the inscription that read: "One can enter the temple only after they are proven worthy and ready to acquire higher knowledge and insights." The higher realms of this knowledge were to initiate the ancient wisdom of the stars and the entire universe through the ancient Initiation System, more commonly known as the Mystery School System. Before anyone was even allowed to step into this sacred education process, the new student was required to purge themselves of any physical, spiritual and mental toxins in their body in preparation for the abundant gifts that the universe had to offer. They also had to undergo a cleansing process which included fasting, meditation and supplication to humble the outer body and manifest their internal prowess. Once this was achieved they had full understanding of their purpose on Earth leading them toward universal prosperity. This process of purging yourself can be seen in today's society through leading a righteous path. This is what we should be aiming for in our own lives, the ability to dwell in the inner temple of our being to know who we truly are.

On the dedication page at the beginning of this book I paid homage to the great ancient divine being that is Djehuti or Thoth as he is more commonly known. It is said that Thoth as a principle was the first great source that all creation myths have since renamed, repacked and called something else. What cannot and should not be denied is the insurmountable idea that Thoth was simply the first prime being created of his own creation, having no beginning and no end, just being. What a wonderful anecdotal revelation that you can think and speak of yourself as something and then become that which you aspire to.

We should begin to see that our journey throughout this book has been a cathartic expedition just like the principle of Thoth. This has been a cycle of revelations, which is by no means a treatise on scientific truths, just mere celestial suggestions. The real question should be: What do you intend to do with this knowledge once you have it? I, for one, have no other intention than to synthesize with universal intelligence and have it ripple throughout the world in which I reside. This may be true for many people, as our true mission should hinge on being harmonious with our own sphere of brilliance, which connects with the rest of the cosmos.

I have learned a great deal while writing this book, not only because it highlighted the retinal detachment in my left eye, but

I have come to realize that had it not been for that event, I most certainly would continue having misguided perceptions. I say that because throughout my life I accepted what I was shown as true without reserving my own judgment. As I began educating myself, I also learned the principles of the universe which made me ask questions about the state of the human experience itself. I was greatly confused at first but then the departure of despair turned into the arrival of awareness. Once I accepted who I am and what I am, being a child of the universe, these principles made me extremely grateful for not losing my sight entirely. Once I adopted this clarity which is now registered in my behavior, my retinal detachment showed me that we as a species are too co-dependent and in a sleep state existence. We do not harness the unique abilities we were born with and we ignore what we had as our core values, like our basic human needs. What we think we need is built on an illusion which is egotistical and does not replicate how our supreme masters used to think or see. The ancient masters taught us that before there was Brahma there was breath and before there was breath there was nothingness. Spiritual gurus know this and we should all set our spiritual sights on the meditative teachings of pure nothing. Hard to accept isn't it? It's difficult to start seeing "no form" when the world you were born into and all imagery were previously constructed for you. Equally difficult is learning the ancient technique of stillness when this world is dependent on so much movement.

So how do we achieve that state of "non-being," stillness and nothingness? In Chapter 2 we looked at the Allegory of the Cave and saw how man can be beguiled into seeing what he is told to see. However, even though it was just a story, there was a period of time when people were in the dark about the powers of the universe. In answer to the question about achieving nothingness, we can give thanks to the resuscitation of our inquisitive mind. Many of us are beginning to understand the laws of abundance and even learning to unlock the mysteries within ourselves. This continuation from where our respected masters departed can only be described as pure enlightenment. When we look through the eyes of great scholars like Lao-Tzu, William Blake, Walt Whitman, Jose Ortega etc. we see that their vision was a foray into how we are the same principle that created our creator. Once we adopt the same intelligence as our ancestors, it will seat us in the universal classroom of prosperity. If we are in Earth's remedial school, when do we graduate? When do I get my certificate to qualify my learning? Well, when I mention graduate I'm not referring to death, I'm referring to your awareness of where you are at any given moment. Our ancestors left spiritual maps for us as monumental clues to learn from. These coordinates allowed us to entertain how brilliant we can truly be. Don't believe me? Just look at the mastery from the Pyramids at Giza to Stonehenge at Salisbury. Ask of your higher self how these monoliths were originally erected and why they cannot be achieved in the same way in today's modern age. Our ancient architects assured freedom once we learned the realms of inter and outer planetary knowledge. Somewhere along the line we forgot to take these teachings and pass on the baton of these feats to unify the human experience. The ancients invested in our knowing, but what they didn't bank on was how the future of mankind would cause so much separation and doubt. We should respect the most celebrated of explorers, namely Howard Carter, who delved into the abyss of curiosity by excavating the sacred statue of Tutankhamun in 1922. Explorers like Carter gave a glimpse of how our ancestors existed, allowing us to feast our eyes on the wonders of the ancient world and their teachings. Even though we might disagree with the disturbance of our ancient structures, these monuments consolidate our reason for being because we are the living reincarnation of the archons that made them. If we are to accept that we are the same thinking material that made the ether of the universe, then what's the difference between the outer realms of the cosmos and us? The universe is made up of a composite of atoms; you too have the same molecular ingredient. So the difference between the universe and us is...that's right, absolutely nothing, no difference at all.

All Eyes on Me

I am writing the end of this chapter somewhere in the first week of January 2014 and I say that because only now has it dawned on me that after years of my own research and observations, we are beginning to meet our pathway to higher learning through a consolidated thought process. Many of today's conscious thought leaders and speakers come equipped with their own version of liberation. Subscribing to their ethos shows that our world has quite an amazing opportunity to repair the higher matrix known as the "consciousness grid." This will greatly make Earth harmonious with herself again, which was always the plan set by our ancient masters although it will take a considerable amount of unified effort.

I could write more on the aspects of the eye and give scholastic evidence on how our luminaries, philosophers and gurus thought. I would welcome being able to illustrate how many spiritual gurus revealed the mysteries of the universe to their pupils. Perhaps one day I will write such angles of study; however, when it comes down to our existence it's our own view that really matters. Okay that's fine Rico, but what's all this talk about the eye and prosperity really been about? I hear you cry! What has it shown us and what's it got to do with me?

The answer is...it has everything to do with you! It should begin to dawn on you by now that you are the mind that makes the universe, and just like the many scholars who accomplished unravelling human perception, you should "speak the password primeval" as suggested by Whitman. Speak as if you are the first prime thought created in all manner of the axiom. You now have a wealth of tools at your disposal to sail off and report what you have discovered, like all great explorers before you. See off into the distance, searching for new vistas and beyond.

I hope you saw this book as an auxiliary to start or continue your own personal journey. I hope it enlightened some of you – heck, I hope it enlightened even one of you! – and I hope it answered some of your questions about the origins of prosperity consciousness. We have had an in-depth look at personal wealth and hopefully I have been successful in showing that authentic power is a pure ambient fusion between our environment and us. All we have to do is humble ourselves and sit at the receiving end of patience. I have been given the opportunity to share my thoughts, my research and my revelations with you through my eye story and for that I am truly grateful. I must admit that I have profited greatly from the lessons of many scholars on the subject of perception. As a result of these teachings, I gained a better perspective about the world in which we live and how to guide things according to my higher self. I most certainly have authentic power now and clarity over my actions. I also learned that anything was possible and, most of all, I learned how to lick my emotional wounds and heal myself.

I am a great believer in the human potential and I acknowledge, as we all should, that there is a higher calling for all of us to step forward and assume the position of awakened beings. However, success, prosperity or being awake will only be revealed when you determine what it means to you personally. What it is not is what you expect to it be, instead it is how you become creative and apply what you know. I say that because we could all travel through life knowing stuff or having supreme intelligence, but I like to think of it like this:

"Knowledge isn't knowledge unless it's applied."

Rico Griffiths-Taitte

If you think you are a fortunate person, having unwavering faith will tell you that you can't be anything else other than prosperous.

This was an eye-opening experience for me being my first book but I'll let you in on a secret: I didn't create the whole concept of 20/20 YOU to highlight having perfect vision, although it is a fitting metaphor about how short-sighted we humans have become. This book not only uses the analogy of sight, 20/20 YOU also refers to a calendar year or period of time to look forward to. Oh yes, we do have an era to look forward to. In the coming years we should start using the phrase "The future looks bright" because like it or not, we are being eclipsed by our own brilliance. We have every resource available to us in connecting with our divine purpose. The time for change is upon us and you can choose to accept it or be destroyed by it. There is a calling for change, even the prophet Sam Cooke told us, "A change is gonna come."

We should set sail from the "out of sight, out of mind" mentality because our enlightened masters hoped that we process their teachings with one expectation. They hoped with crossed fingers that we never forget where we came from. If the years leading up to 20/20 and beyond promise to reveal a huge shift in consciousness for the chosen few, what about our youth, what's in it for them? We can have a greater influence on future generations once we impress upon their mindset to become more proactive. Only through nurturing and guidance can we show them that anything is possible. Remember, all great successes manifest when your thinking is larger than you expect. We should be teaching our children "don't just dream big, have big dreams."

In recent times there has been evidence of our careers having pandemic uncertainty in the workplace, creating a rapid decline in morale. We can see this especially when we look at the current loss and restructuring of our jobs, which shows there is no such thing as job security anymore. The ambiguity of living pay-check to pay-check illustrates that our livelihoods are suffering from economic cataracts. In order to be prosperous we should follow the rules set by our ancestors in changing our mind's eye with corrective surgery. This means, we the seekers of the truth should start looking at our future through clearer spectacles that can make our lives spec-ta-cular.

We have learned in this book new ways of thinking but let me ask you this: Is it really new? No, however, it is refreshing, like the spinning dance of the Sufi who generates a heightened state of tranquility and awareness in one continuous turn. You see, dear friend, that's how consciousness moves, in cycles. The cosmic twirl of consciousness is universal balance, for what goes around must come back around. How this new perspective will impact our future generations, I guess we'll have to wait and see...

Final Thoughts

Seeing the Light of Day

Chapter 13:

Final Thoughts

What a journey of self-discovery, seen through the eyes of ancient intent. We have revealed that our pathway to prosperity has significant portholes of brilliance already embedded in our DNA. However, this is just the beginning. This information is now at your disposal any time you require it and I hope you have been inspired to challenge your own perceptions so that you can unlock the codes to improve your life. Not just to benefit personally, but make a difference to those around you also. You have a great foundation of enlightening tools to set an example to your children and society, burgeoning on affecting generations to follow.

People have been blinded by the information that you now hold in your lexicon. I don't mean that in a non-productive sense but it seems that only initiated people are privy to the formulae of prosperity. Those fortunate ones are already sharing similar concepts through the speed of the information superhighway, otherwise known as the Internet. This means we are all just a click away from accessing knowledge that had been hidden from us before. Your intention is of paramount importance when seeking prosperity and success. It takes many deciding factors to achieve what you want including sacrifice, courage, reverence and gratitude to name a few. I have seen countless entrepreneurs make millions by using these principles, but I've also seen millions of people become frustrated by misusing it.

Seeing the Light of Day

I have been called many things in my life, some of which would be too rude to say here; however, I am grateful in being called a thought leader on creative expression. I like to think that I have acquired the knowledge of "one who is awake" as the Buddha described when asked, "What does it means to be enlightened?" First of all, before anything else, I am a student. I am only a master or expert on that which I know, for I am an expert on the subject of being me. The teachings that are the key to my liberation were founded in being among my elders. I spent a great deal of my upbringing with my mother and grandparents. We were very resourceful in those days. We certainly were not financially wealthy but I would like to think that we have never been poor. My childhood was filled with life lessons, like my mother and grandma teaching me how to cook and sharing ways of the ancients and Caribbean culture. In fact I'll go as far as to say that those lessons taught me how to appreciate that our situation wasn't poor, it was pure.

I was shown that food was love, especially the preparation of it, and togetherness was love and respect was paramount. So I guess I have always been prosperous which has guided me my whole life. When I recall the life lessons from my mother and elders it serves to improve my connection to my inner intelligence. Through my daily acknowledgment of my ancestors I have learned to forgive my previous failings and I allow myself to continually evolve. This has afforded me to have complete commune with my purpose.

I cannot recommend the principles displayed in this book highly enough because throughout history ordinary people lived extraordinary lives from these revelations. They discovered that if they adopted these ancient principles and changed their perspective, they could unlock their own mystery and most certainly grow to become prosperous.

"Happiness is neither virtue nor pleasure nor this thing nor that but simply growth, we are happy when we are growing."

William Butler Yeats

We must reinforce the idea that in order to achieve our goals there is nothing external of self that apprehends us. On this planet called Earth School I don't know when I'll finally graduate. I'm still here which means I'm still learning. I sincerely hope that you see your own truth by changing your perceptions to know yourself and become truly prosperous.

Procul His (Beyond these things)

"When consciousness is transformed, things begin to happen. Man begins to operate differently, begins to think differently, begins to see differently, he begins to feel differently, and, seeing differently and feeling differently makes a tremendous difference to what you become. Make no mistake about it."

Dr. Ivan Van Sertima

Acknowledgments

Along my path there have been many lessons with just as many teachers who showed me all the tools needed to be a student of enlightenment. This guidance was started by the awesome goddess power of my mother Patricia Griffiths because had it not been for her then I most certainly would not be able to shine prosperously. I thank you Mum for the breath of life and assistance for turning me into a soldier of truth and defender of ancient knowledge. Your support is the epitome of divine grace and personal value. You have been the highest pillar of prosperity and I will always embody your teachings. Although I never really said this before, because it goes beyond words, on both the physical and spiritual realms...I love you.

I thank the medical profession at Moorfields Eye Hospital for their expertise throughout my eye condition. I would like to send a special thanks to Gareth of Authoright for resuscitating my message and giving me the exposure that I needed to share my vision. Your expertise is invaluable as is your friendship and belief in my abilities, thank you.

A massive thank you to Mr. Stevie Wonder for showing me that I didn't need external vision to see internal prowess. I especially would like to thank all those who found a platform to speak the truth about inner vision. I acknowledge every speaker who ever braved the stage to share his or her message, most notably Keith Harrell, Les Brown, Victor Antonio Gonzales, Zig Ziglar, Stephen Covey, Anthony Robbins, Brendon Burchard, Melanie Duncan and Eric Thomas to name a few.

I would like to pay particular homage to all the ancient deities and luminaries of Ancient Egypt, otherwise known as Kemet and beyond. There are way too many to mention here but to those whom I praise daily, known and unknown, called and uncalled, I sincerely thank you.

And lastly, I would be doing a great injustice if I did not thank the metaphysicians who showed me the path to those ancient deities so I could study their teachings and pass on the baton of this knowledge with purpose. So without further delay, thank you to Doctor Na'im Akbar, Asa Hilliard, Ivan Van Sertima, Gerald Massey, Dr. Francis Cress Wilson, Phil Valentine, Bobby Hemmit, Dr. Delbert Blair to name a few. Thank you, thank you, thank you. When I had nowhere else to turn to validate what I had been feeling since my youth, you provided a space for students like me to know thyself.

About the Author

Rico was born in London, England to Caribbean parents although he has always felt a connection to his ancient cultural heritage. Rico has had a fascination with art since childhood and as a teenager had aspirations of working in the animation industry. He had been working in the corporate world for many years before being diagnosed with having a detached retina in 1998. This led to a powerful revelation which guided him to study ancient philosophies, coupled with the life-changing messages from Stevie Wonder's album Innervisions. Rico's self-discovery gave him the inspiration to see how others could change their own lives and experiences through ancient perspectives.

Rico has since become an accredited Neuro-Linguistic Programer, personal development coach, etymologist and metaphysician. He has extensive experience of personal and performance management and is an authority on ancient views of prosperity.

Since starting up his own business in 2008 he has given clients exclusive clarity on leadership by facilitating personal development programs. He now represents inner power, which is present in all of us to overcome life's challenges.

He cites: "In order to achieve our goals there is nothing external of ourselves that apprehends us; we need to look inside our own being for an intuitive revelation."

www.ricopharao.com
www.ricopharaoshop.com
www.facebook.com/rico.griffithstaitte
uk.linkedin.com/in/synergyreality

Bibliography

"Man may not know truth but he can embody it".
William Butler Yeats *(1865 – 1939)*
Irish poet, playwright and mystic
Letter to Lady Elizabeth Pelham (January 4, 1939)

"There is no truth until you decide what truth is".
Dr. Delbert Blair *(dates undisclosed)*
Terrestrials, Extraterrestrials and Aliens Lectures

"Life isn't about finding yourself, life is about creating yourself".
George Bernard Shaw *(July 26, 1856 – Nov 2, 1950)*
Irish playwright and winner of the Nobel Prize for Literature in 1925

"Never allow someone to be your priority while allowing yourself to be their option".
Mark Twain *(Nov 30, 1835 – April 21, 1910)*
American author and humorist

"It is the teaching that all is Spirit, and matter is not obedient shadow-picturing thereof, which is the final subtle message toward me that makes me see that I AM what I AM and alter not. Spirit is the gentle Mother doctrine among the doctrines of the world — gentle but inexorable. She brings to exposure the Man Child, my I AM who shall rule all nations with a rod of iron. The iron that is strongest is magnetic. It rules in the earth by holding all the particles together.

It rules in the sun. It rules in all the spheres. They roll because of the magnet. So all my being has moved because of my I AM. So all my universe shall wheel to my ordination.

"This is my ministry. I am glad to give myself to my Self and to give all my world to my Self and let my Self do in judgment twelve works upon the earth.

This is my ministry. I have heard all I shall ever hear. I know all I shall ever know. I now make my Self known.

I make my Self known by speaking, thinking, writing and living the word of my Self — my I AM".
Emma Curtis Hopkins *(1849 – 1925)*
American spiritual author and leader

"All causes are essentially mental, and whosoever comes into daily contact with a high order of thinking must take on some of it".
Charles Fillmore *(August 22, 1854 – July 5, 1948)*
American mystic

"When the student is ready the master teacher will appear".
Ancient proverb

"There are things known and there are things unknown, and in between are the doors of perception".
Aldous Huxley *(1894 – 1963)*
English writer

"I cannot shut myself up within the realm of science. All my knowledge of the world, even my scientific knowledge, is gained from my own particular point of view, or from some experience of the world without which the symbols of science would be meaningless".... *"I am, not a 'living creature' nor even a 'man', nor again even 'a consciousness' endowed with all the characteristics which zoology, social anatomy or inductive psychology recognize in these various products of the natural or historical process – I am the absolute source, my existence does not stem from my antecedents, from my physical and social environment; instead it moves out toward them and sustains them, for I alone bring into being for myself".*

Maurice Merleau-Ponty *(1908 – 1961)*
French phenomenological philosopher

"Whether you think you can or you think you can't, you're right".
Henry Ford *(1863 – 1947)*
American industrialist

"Courage is resistance to fear, mastery of fear, not absence of fear".
Mark Twain *(Nov 30, 1835 – April 21, 1910)*
American author and humorist

Alice:	*"Oh, no, no. I was just wondering if you could help me find my way."*
Cheshire Cat:	*"Well that depends on where you want to get to."*
Alice:	*"Oh, it really doesn't matter, as long as..."*
Cheshire Cat:	*"Then it really doesn't matter which way you go."*

Lewis Carroll
From the 1865 novel **Alice in Wonderland**

"Self-knowledge can be obtained only by looking into the mind and virtue of the soul, which is the diviner part of a man, as we see our own image in another's eye".

Plato *(circa 428 BC – circa 348 BC)*

Taken from the first conversations between Plato's Dialogues with Alcibiades

"Believe nothing, no matter where you read it, or who said it, even if I have said it, unless it agrees with your own reason and your own common sense".

Buddha

"When you come into the life just as yourself, surrendered and open, you're not a program not on some mission, you just are".

Mooji (1954 – present)

Spiritual guru and teacher

"Your sense of self comes not from thought but the stillness of thought. The presence which comes out of consciousness of who you are. Once you know who you are at this moment, your life situation is of relative importance. It is of relative importance whether you are poor or wealthy, if the body is healthy, if you have satisfying relationships, whether you have a nice place to live or an unpleasant place to live, it all has importance but it is not of absolute importance. Know who you are beyond the forms".

Eckhart Tolle *(1948 – present)*

Spiritual teacher

"Everyone thinks of changing the world, but no one thinks of changing himself".

Leo Tolstoy *(1828 – 1910)*

Taken from Leo Tolstoy's Pamphlets

"When you take one step toward the Guru, he takes a million steps toward you".
Sikh saying

"When people see your personality come out, they feel so good, like they actually know who you are".
Usain Bolt *(1986 – present)*
Jamaican sprinter

"Living is a constant process of deciding what to do".
Jose Ortega *(1883 – 1955)*
José Ortega y Gasset, Spanish liberal philosopher

Luke Skywalker: *"I won't fail you, I'm not afraid."*
Yoda: *"Good, you will be, you will be."*
Stars Wars Episode V: The Empire Strikes Back (1980)

"The only way to keep from going backward is to keep going forward. Eternal vigilance is the price of success. There are three steps, and each one is absolutely essential. You must first have the knowledge of your power; second, the courage to dare; third, the faith to do".
Charles F. Haanel *(1866 – 1949)*
American New Thought author

"Peace can be reached through meditation on the knowledge which dreams give. Peace can also be reached through concentration upon that which is dearest to the heart".
Patanjali Indian saint

"You can't depend on your eyes when your imagination is out of focus".
Mark Twain *(Nov 30, 1835 – April 21, 1910)*
American author and humorist

"Happiness cannot be traveled to, owned, earned, worn or consumed. Happiness is the spiritual experience of living every minute with love, grace and gratitude".
Denis Waitley *(1933 – present)*
American motivational speaker and writer

"Let us be grateful to people who make us happy; they are the charming gardeners who make our souls blossom".
Marcel Proust *(1871 – 1922)*
French novelist

"Be in a state of gratitude for everything that shows up in your life. Be thankful for the storms as well as the smooth sailing. What is the lesson or gift in what you are experiencing right now? Find your joy not in what's missing in your life but in how you can serve."
Wayne Dyer *(May 10, 1940 – present)*
Self-help author and motivational speaker

Neo: "I can't go back, can I?"
Morpheus: "No. But if you could, would you really want to?"
The Matrix 1999 movie

"Neo, sooner or later you're going to realize just as I did that there's a difference between knowing the path and walking the path".
Morpheus - The Matrix 1999 movie

"Awakening is possible only for those who seek it and want it, for those who are ready to struggle with themselves and work on themselves for a very long time and very persistently in order to attain it".
G. I. Gurdjieff *(1866 – 1949)*
Influential spiritual teacher

"Happiness is neither virtue nor pleasure nor this thing nor that but simply growth, we are happy when we are growing".
William Butler Yeats *(1865 – 1939)*
Irish poet, playwright

"When consciousness is transformed, things begin to happen. Man begins to operate differently, begins to think differently, begins to see differently, he begins to feel differently, and, seeing differently and feeling differently makes a tremendous difference to what you become. Make no mistake about it."
Dr. Ivan Van Sertima *(Jan 26, 1935 – May 25, 2009)*
Taken from the 1986 lecture given by Dr. Ivan Van Sertima at Camden Town Hall, London

Testimonials

"Rico is a talented visionary coach who brings enlightening techniques to his clients with industry expertise and ancient insight. He is unique as he is gifted at helping people empower themselves. For us at the BBC Club, Rico has been a valuable asset in coaching and mentoring our clients".

Sachin Gangwal – BBC Club

"If it's value, self resolution and the truth that you're after, you just found it".

Martin Gayle – BCP, Entrepreneur

"I initially didn't understand what I needed from coaching through ancient wisdom. But just after one session with Rico, he guided me to see things from a whole new point of view. I consider myself to be a savvy person, although through Rico's knowledge in identifying today's problems, he left me wanting to learn more about the world we live. His ancient perspective quickly and effectively gave me tools to address concerns that I faced daily. With his help, I was able to recognize where I could improve myself and my peers. I see Rico as someone who has taken the time to analyze human behaviour and because of his teachings I found balance and felt completely in the presence of one who knows".

Eli Coory – Journalist

"Mr Rico Griffiths – Taitte has worked tirelessly/single-mindedly for you to embrace this knowledge with an open mind, a sturdy body (to take on the impact of these powerful words!) and a spiritually aware soul, all becoming whole, for the (third) eye to see, and the mind to feed…"

Shakiyla Brown – BBAF

"I myself am a personal coach and I find that within the empowerment industry, so many people are beating the phrase "New thought leader" to death. During my time with rico, I was required to make a very difficult decision in my career and family. With his help, Rico playfully showed me that "New Thought" is the same old patterns that had been ignored. With Rico it became an easy transition to stop kidding myself and start creating the life that I had desired. My only regret is I wish I had found rico sooner".

Mila Sanchez – Brazilian Executive Coach

"Rico taught me not just one but all the laws of the universe".

Zephryn – Actor

"Communication is the key within every business. I felt that there was definitely a communication breakdown between my colleagues in my team. Rico was flexible and empowering with his guidance. He identified the lack of cohesion in our company and proved that we had to enlist the "EDGE" in our vision. He modified our approach with a refreshing look at our working environment. He is now catching the attention of other teams who have seen a massive turnaround in our sales department. I can't thank you enough for the impact that you have made to our business".

Jerry Ines, Team – Leader of Planet X Productions

"Working with Rico made me look upon his coaching method as transformational. He was an attentive listener, mentor and foremost solution-based visionary who helped me identify the challenges I was having. He is an absolute visionary expert who shows humility whilst displaying an authority in personal development. Thanks again"

Kevin Simms – Musician, Entrepreneur

"I now know the difference between good coaching and even greater guidance. Rico showed me how to continue on the path to greater success personally and professionally. He taught me about the techniques from ancient masters and how they continually work through me. I had read and understood the law of attraction however, before I met Rico I really didn't know how to apply it".

Angela Belvett – Coordinator

www.ingramcontent.com/pod-product-compliance
Lightning Source LLC
LaVergne TN
LVHW041213080426
835508LV00011B/944